I0127752

Microplastics removal and wastewater recycling with membrane & ozone technology

Milenko Roš, Jolanda Rihter Pikl
Hakim El Khiar, Nataša Uranjek

Title: Microplastics removal and wastewater recycling with membrane & ozone technology

ISBN: 978-1-63902-821-4

Author: Milenko Roš, Jolanda Rihter Pikl, Hakim El Khiar, Nataša Uranjek

Cover image: https://pixabay.com/

Publisher: Generis Publishing
Online orders: www.generis-publishing.com
Contact email: info@generis-publishing.com

Microplastics removal and wastewater recycling with membrane & ozone technology

Milenko Roš, Jolanda Rihter Pikl, Hakim El Khiar, Nataša Uranjek

Table of contents

1 Introduction

In wastewater treatment, the reuse of treated wastewater and the complete disposal of suspended solids have been mentioned frequently. These include microplastics, increasing in wastewater and treated water (effluent from treatment plants). It also contains microplastics, which are increasingly occurring in wastewater and treated water (effluent from wastewater treatment plants).

To prepare water for reuse, removing organic matter and harmful substances as much as possible beforehand is essential. It is possible to do with good membrane filtration and disinfection.

The book is organised into the following Chapters: Filtration; Disinfection; Microplastics; Membrane filtration and ozonation system; Application of SiC membrane filtration; Municipal wastewater treatment with membrane filtration and ozonation; Industrial wastewater treatment using SiC membrane filtration; Conclusions; and Literature.

The chapter on filtration shows the basis of surface filtration, depth filtration membrane filtration, and exceptional SiC membrane filtration. In the chapter on disinfection, we discuss the mechanism of disinfectants, factors influencing the action of disinfectants, and different disinfection systems (disinfection with chlorine, chlorine with chlorine compounds, UV disinfection, and disinfection with ozone). The chapter on microplastics are described the main characteristics of microplastics. The chapter on membrane filtration and ozonation system describes the pilot plant for wastewater treatment with membrane filtration with ozonation. In the chapter Application of SiC membrane are described examples of SiC membrane filtration. The last two chapters discuss examples of membrane filtration in the treatment of municipal and industrial wastewater. In the end, we collected literature, which we used in the preparation of the book and our scientific research findings.

2 Filtration

Filtration (Tchobanoglous et al., 2003) is a mechanical or physical process used to separate solids and liquid phases (water) by passing through a specific filter (medium). Water and particles smaller than the pore size of the filter can pass through the filter. Since the medium can be vastly different, but we can also use various media thicknesses, we distinguish according to the principle of operation of the following filtrations:

- surface filtration,
- depth filtration , and
- membrane filtration.

2.1 Surface filtration

Surface filtration (Figure 1) (Gunt, 2021) involves removing solid suspended solids from a liquid by mechanical sieving so that the fluid passes through a mechanical barrier (filter material). The material used for the mechanical barrier (filter material) is made of paper, different fabrics, or different synthetic materials. The filter material has a pore size of 10 to 30 µm or more.

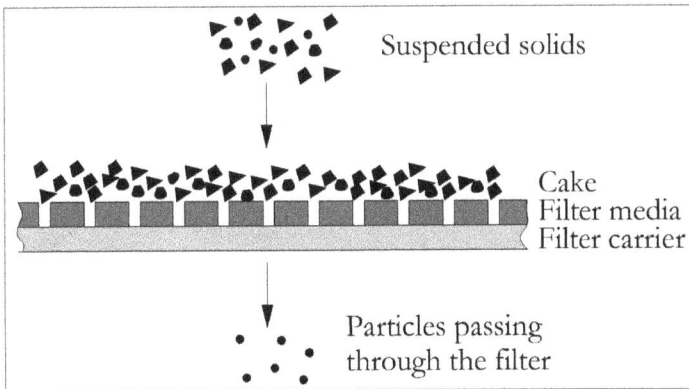

Figure 1: Scheme of the surface filtration process

Surface filtration could be successful if a layer of filter material called a cake is formed above the filter. The mixture of water and solids flows through the cake and the filter (e.g., filter presses).

In water or wastewater treatment processes, surface filtration is used for various purposes, such as:

- for removal of residues of suspended solids from discharges of biological treatment plants or stabilization lagoons,
- for separation of activated sludge and water suspension,
- for separation of particles formed during Physical-chemical cleaning, e.g., in coagulation or flocculation.

Examples of filtration are shown in the following figures: Figure 2 and Figure 3.

Figure 2: Filter press

Figure 3: Belt press for removing water from mixed liquor suspended solids (detail)

2.2 Depth filtration

Deep filtration (Gunt, 2021) involves removing solids suspended in a liquid, bypassing the liquid through a filter pad containing granular or compressible material (Figure 4). Although depth filtration is one of the basic units used to prepare drinking water, filtration of effluents from wastewater treatment processes is becoming more widespread. Deep filtration is now used to achieve additional removal of suspended solids (including solid BOD from effluents from biological or physicochemical processes, to reduce solids emissions and, perhaps more importantly, as a preparatory step to allow effective disinfection of the filtered effluent. Deep filtration is also used as a pre-treatment step for membrane filtration. Single-stage or two-stage filtration is also used to remove chemically precipitated phosphorus. The first depth filter was developed for wastewater treatment as a slow sand filter (typical filtration rate is between 30 and 60 m^3 / m^2.day). A fast sand filter, which is now more in use (the typical filtration rate is between 80 and 200 m^3 / m^2.day), has been developed for larger volumes of water.

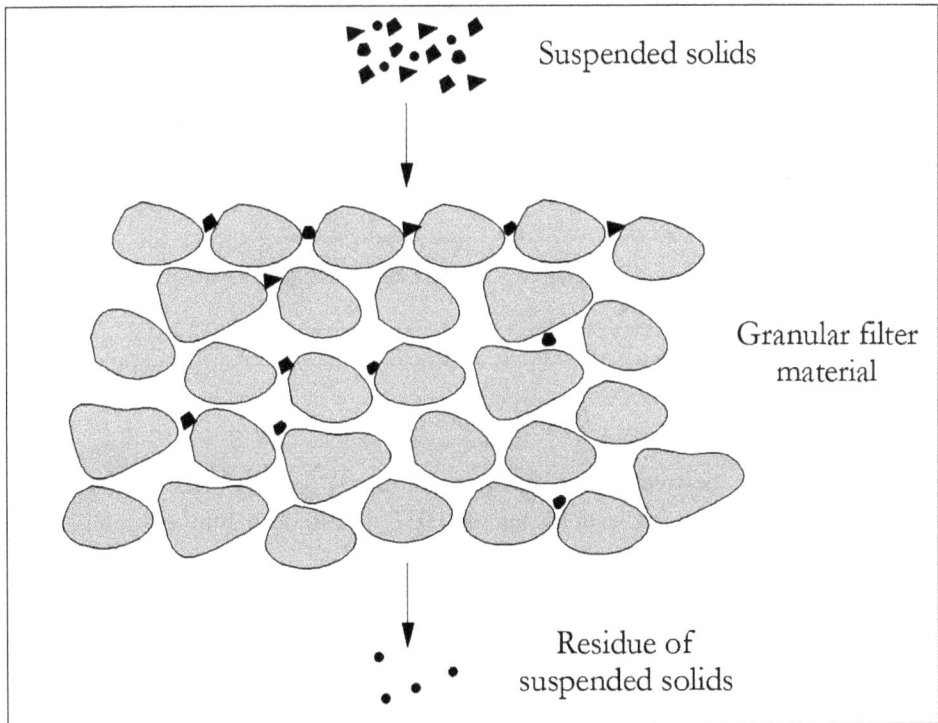

Figure 4: Scheme of the deep filtration process

Process description

During filtration in a conventional filter, where water flows from the top to down, polluted water flows to the top of the filter (Figure 5). When water passes through a filter, suspended solids are removed by various mechanisms such as filtration, sedimentation, interaction, interception, adhesion, flocculation, chemical adsorption, physical adsorption, or biological growth. After a specific time, when the filter is saturated (filled with substituted substances), the filtration starts to slow down until it stops completely. However, the quality of filtered water may start to deteriorate. In both cases, the filter must be washed with clean water from the bottom upwards (in the opposite direction of the filtration process). Rinse with return water has two purposes. First, the suspended solids are washed from the filter material, and second, the filter material (sand) is loosened, and the filter usually becomes flowable again.

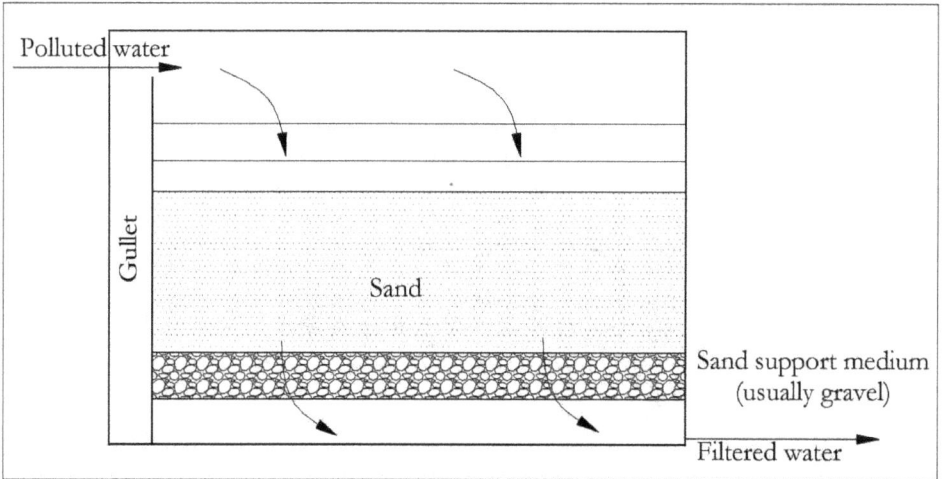

Figure 5: Sand filter

The pore size between the filter material (sand) depends on the size of the material. Sand with a particle diameter of 0.037 mm to 25.4 mm is usually used, depending on the need for filtration.

2.3 Membrane filtration

With classical filtration, solid and partially colloidal particles can be removed from the water. With membrane filtration (Schlosser, 2014), the filtration area expands to significantly smaller particles, including dissolved matter, depending on the size of the pores through which the water is filtered (filter pores are from 0.0001 to 1.0 µm).

14

The role of membrane filtration is to use special (selective) membranes that allow the passage of only certain substances present in the liquid (Figure 6).

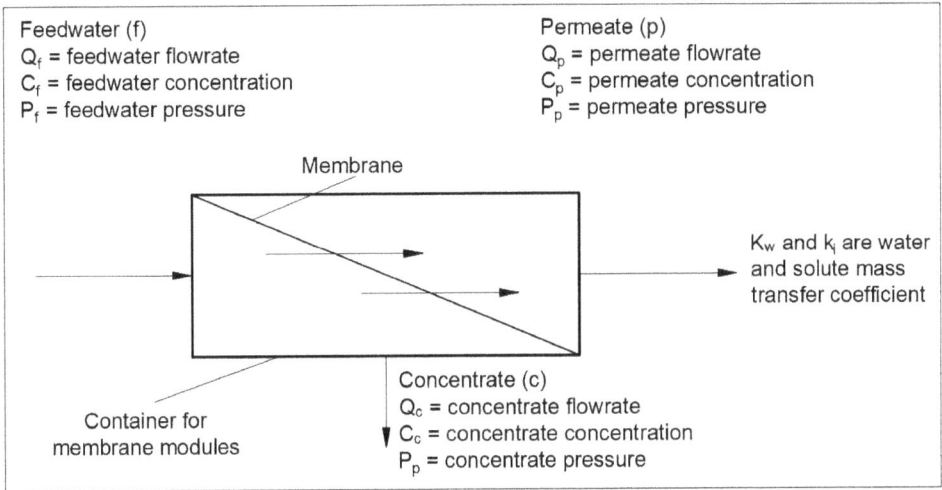

Feedwater (f)
Q_f = feedwater flowrate
C_f = feedwater concentration
P_f = feedwater pressure

Permeate (p)
Q_p = permeate flowrate
C_p = permeate concentration
P_p = permeate pressure

Membrane

K_w and k_l are water and solute mass transfer coefficient

Container for membrane modules

Concentrate (c)
Q_c = concentrate flowrate
C_c = concentrate concentration
P_p = concentrate pressure

Figure 6: Definition of membrane process

Membrane processes include microfiltration (MF), ultrafiltration (UF), nanofiltration (nF), reverse osmosis (RO), dialysis, and electrodialysis (ed). Membrane processes can also be divided into other ways, which include:

- the type of material from which the membrane is made,
- the nature of the driving force,
- separation mechanism, and
- nominal particle sizes achieved by separation.

The general properties of membrane processes, including separation zones, are shown in the following table (Table 1).

Table 1: General characteristics of membrane processes

Membrane process	Membrane driving force	Typical separation mechanism	Typical operation range (µm)	Typical constituents removed
Microfiltration	Hydrostatic pressure difference or vacuum in an open vessel	Sieve	0.08-2.0	Total suspended solids, turbidity, protozoan oocysts, some bacteria, and viruses
Ultrafiltration	Hydrostatic pressure difference	Sieve	0.005-0.2	Macromolecules, colloids, most bacteria, some viruses, and proteins
Nanofiltration	Hydrostatic pressure difference	Sieve + (solution/diffusion + exclusion)	0.001—0.01	Small molecules, some hardness, viruses
Reverse osmosis	Hydrostatic pressure difference	Solution/diffusion + exclusion	0.0001-0.001	Very small molecules, colour, hardness, sulphates, nitrates, sodium, other ions
Dialysis	Concentration's difference	Diffusion	-	Macromolecules, colloids, most bacteria, some viruses, proteins
Electrodialysis	Electromotive force	Ion exchange with selective membranes	-	Ionised salt ions

Membrane materials

Membranes used to treat water or wastewater typically consist of a thin skin having a thickness of about 0.2 to 0.25 µm supported by a more porous structure about 100 µm in thickness. Most commercial membranes are produced as flat sheets, fine hollow fibres, or tubular form. The flat sheets are two types, asymmetric and composite. Asymmetric membranes are cast in the ion process and consist of a very thin (less than 1µm) layer and a thicker (up to 100 µm) porous layer that adds support and is capable of high-water flux. Thin-film composite (TFC) membranes are made by bonding a thin cellulose acetate, polyamide, or another active layer (typically 0.15 to

0.25 µm thick) to a thicker, porous substrate, which provides stability. Membranes can be made from several different organic and inorganic materials. The membranes used for wastewater treatment are typically organic. The principal types of membranes used include polypropylene, cellulose acetate, aromatic polyamides, and thin-film composite (TFC). The choice of membrane and system configuration is based on minimising membrane clogging and deterioration, typically based on pilot plant studies.

Driving force

The distinguishing characteristic of the first four membrane processes considered in Table 1 (MF, UF, NF, and RO) is the application of hydraulic pressure to bring about the desired separation. Where MF membrane elements are submerged in an open vessel, vacuum is used instead of pressure. Dialysis involves the transport of constituents through a semipermeable membrane based on concentration differences. Electrodialysis involves the use of an electromotive force and ion-selective membranes to accomplish the separation of charged ionic species.

Removal mechanisms

The separation of particles in MF and UF is accomplished primarily by straining (sieving). In NF and RO, tiny particles are rejected by the water layer adsorbed on the surface of the membrane, which is known as a *dense* membrane. Ionic species are transported across the membrane by diffusion through the pores of the macromolecules comprising the membrane. Typically, NF can be used to reject constituents as small as 0.001 µm, whereas RO can reject particles as small as 0.0001 µm. Straining is also crucial in NF membranes, especially at larger pore size openings.

Size of separation

The pore sizes in the membranes are identified as macropores (>50 nm), mesopores (2 to 50 nm), and micropores (<2 nm). Because the pore sizes in RO are so small, the membranes are defined as dense. In Figure 7, there is considerable overlap in the size of the particles removed, especially between NF in RO. Nanofiltration is used most in water-softening operations in place of chemical precipitation.

Aqueous salts
Humic acids
Colloidal material
Viruses
small organic monmers, sugars, pesticides, herbicides
Bacteral cells
Cell fragments and debris
Range for TSS test
Conventional depth filtration

Microfiltration (MF)
Ultrafiltration (UF)
Nanofiltration (NF)
Reverse osmosis (RO)

| 10^{-4} | 10^{-3} | 10^{-2} | 10^{-1} | 0 | 10 | 10^2 | 10^3 |

Particle size, μm

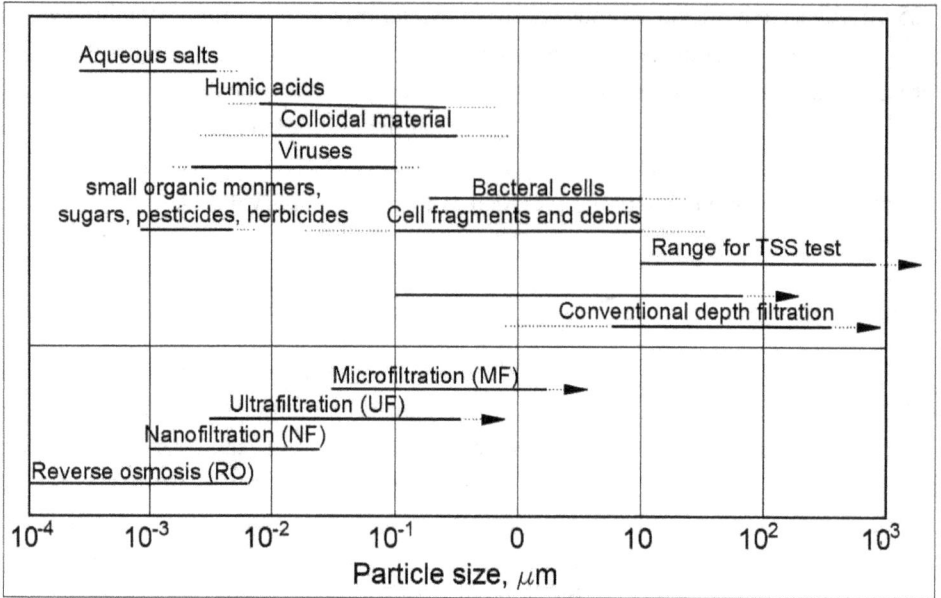

Figure 7: Comparison of the size of constituents found in wastewater and operating size ranges for membrane technologies.

Membrane configuration

In the membrane field, the term *module* is used to describe a complete unit comprised of the membranes, the pressure support structure for the membrane, the feed inlet and outlet permeate and retentate ports, and an overall support structure. The principal types of membrane modules used for water and wastewater treatment are (1) tubular, (2) hollow fibre, and (3) spiral wound. Plates and frame and pleated cartridge filters are also available but are used commonly in industrial applications.

Tabular modules. In the tabular configuration, the membrane is cast on the inside of a support tube. Many tubes (either singly or in a bundle) are then placed in an appropriate pressure vessel. The concentrate continues to flow through the feed tube. These units are generally used for water with high suspended solids or plugging potential. Tubular units are the easiest to clean, which is accomplished by circulating chemicals and pumping a "foamball" or "spongeball" to wipe the membrane mechanically. Tubular units produce at a low production rate relative to their volume, and the membranes are generally expensive.

Hollow fibre. The hollow-fibre membrane module consists of a bundle of hundreds to thousands of hollow fibres. The entire assembly is inserted into a pressure vessel. The feed can be applied to the inside of the fibre (inside-outflow) or outside the fibre (outside-in flow).

Spiral wound. In the spiral-wound membrane, a flexible permeate spacer is placed between two flat membrane sheets. The membranes are sealed on three sides. The open side is attached to a perforated pipe. A flexible feed spacer is added, and the flat sheet is rolled into a tight circular configuration. Thin-film composites are used most commonly in spiral-wound membrane modules. The term spiral derives from the fact that the flow in the rolled-up arrangement of membranes and support sheets follows a spiral pattern.

2.3.1 Membrane processes

The operation of membrane processes is quite simple. A pump is used to pressurize the feed solution (water or wastewater) and circulate it through the module. A valve is used to maintain the pressure of the retentate. The permeate is withdrawn, typically at atmospheric pressure. As constituents in the feed water accumulate on the membranes (often terms membrane fouling), the pressure builds up on the feed side, the membrane flux (i. e., flow-through membrane) starts to decrease, and the per cent rejection also starts to decrease. When the performance has deteriorated to a given level, the membrane modules are taken out of service and backwashed and/or cleaned chemically. The operational configuration and parameters for the various membrane processes are considered.

2.3.1.1 Microfiltration and ultrafiltration

Three different process configurations are used with microfiltration and ultrafiltration units (Aani et al., 2020; Anis et al., 2019), as illustrated in Figure 8. In the first configuration, known as crossflow (Figure 8 a), the feedwater is pumped with a crossflow tangential to the membrane. Water that does not pass through the membrane is recirculated through the membrane after blending with additional feedwater. The second configuration, also known as crossflow (Figure 8 b), is similar to the first, except that the water does not pass through the membrane is recirculated to a storage reservoir. The third configuration is known as direct feed (also *dead-end*) (Figure 8 c) in that there is no crossflow. All water applied to the membrane passes through the membrane. Raw feed water is used periodically to flush the accumulated material from the membrane surface.

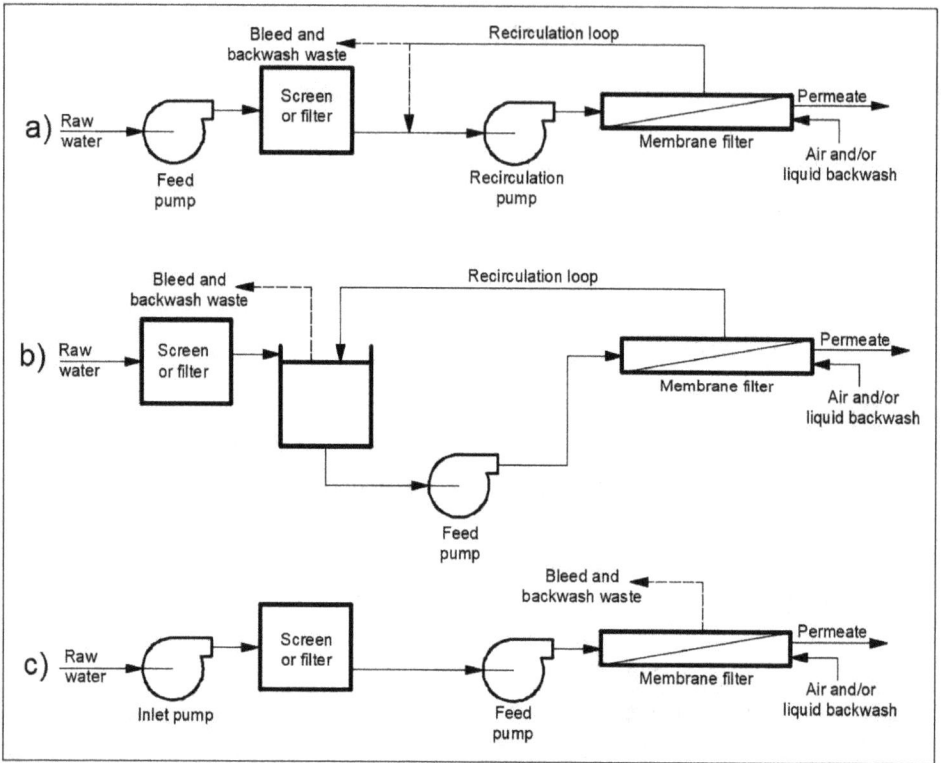

Figure 8: Typical operational modes for MF and UF membrane processes: (a) cross flow, (b) cross flow with reservoir, and (c) direct feed

For the crossflow mode of operation (Figure 8 a, and Figure 8 b), the transmembrane pressure is given by the following expression:

$$P_m = \left[\frac{P_f + P_c}{2}\right] - P_p$$

Where is:

P_m = transmembrane pressure gradient, kPa

P_f = inlet pressure of feed stream, kPa

P_p = pressure of permeate stream, kPa

The overall pressure drop across the filter module for the crossflow mode of operation is given by:

20

$$P = P_f - P_p$$

Where is:

P = pressure drop across the module, kPa

P_f = inlet pressure of feed stream, kPa

P_p = pressure of permeate stream, kPa

For the direct-feed mode of operation (Figure 8 c) the transmembrane pressure is given by the following expression:

$$P_m = P_f - P_p$$

Where is:

P_m = pressure drop across the module, kPa

P_f = inlet pressure of feed stream, kPa

P_p = pressure of permeate stream, kPa

The total permeate flow from a membrane system is given by:

$$Q_p = F_w A$$

Where is:

Q_p = permeate stream flowrate, kg/s

F_w = transmembrane water flux rate, kg/m².s

A = membrane area, m²

As would be expected, the transmembrane water flux rate is a function of the quality of the feed stream, the degree of retreatment, the characteristics of the membrane, and the system operating parameters.

The recovery rate r is defined as:

$$r = \frac{Q_p}{Q_f} \times 100$$

Where is:

r = recovery rate, %

Q_p = permeate stream flow, kg/s

Q_f = feed stream flow, kg/s

It should be noted that there is a difference in the recovery rate (which refers to the water) and the rate of rejection (which refers to the solute) as given below:

$$R, \% = \frac{C_f - C_p}{C_f} \times 100 = 1 - \frac{C_p}{C_f} \times 100$$

The corresponding mass balance equations are:

$$Q_f = Q_p + Q_c$$

$$Q_f C_f = Q_p C_p + Q_c C_c$$

Three different operation modes can be used to control the operation of a membrane process concerning flux and transmembrane pressure (TMP). The three modes illustrated in Figure 9, are (1) constant flux in which the flux rate is fixed and the TMP allowed to vary (increase) with time; (2) constant TMP in which the TMP is fixed and the flux rate is allowed to vary (decrease) with time; and (3) both the flux rate and TMP are allowed to vary with time. Traditionally, the constant-flux mode of operation has been used. However, based on the results of a recent study with various wastewater effluents, it appears the mode in which both the flux rate and the TMP are allowed to vary with time may be the most effective mode of operation.

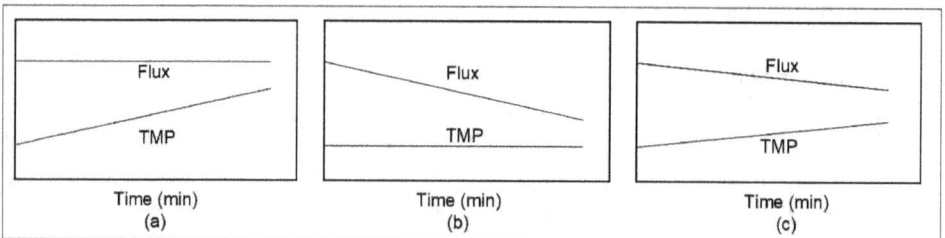

Figure 9: Three modes of membrane operation: (a) constant flux, (b) constant pressure, and (c) nonrestricted flux and pressure

2.3.1.2 Reverse osmosis

When the semipermeable membrane separates two solutions with different solute concentrations, a difference in chemical potential will exist across the membrane (Figure 10).

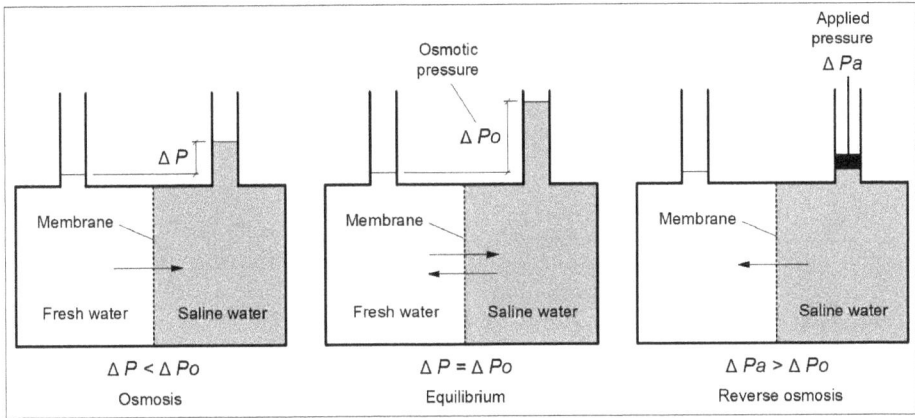

Figure 10: Definition sketch of osmotic flow: (a) osmotic flow, (b) osmotic equilibrium, and (c) reverse osmosis.

Water will tend to diffuse through the membrane from the lower concentration (higher-potential) side to the higher-concentration (lower-potential) side. In a finite volume system, flow continues until the pressure difference balances the chemical potential difference. This balancing pressure difference is termed the *osmotic pressure* and is a function of the solute characteristics, concentration, and temperature. If a pressure gradient opposite in direction and more significant than the osmotic pressure is imposed across the membrane, flow from the more concentrated to the less concentrated region will occur and is termed *reverse osmosis* (see Figure 10 c)

Many different models have been developed to determine the surface area of the membrane and the number of arrays required (Figure 11). The basic equations used to develop the various models are as follows. The flux of water through the membrane is a function of the pressure gradient:

$$F_w = k_w(\Delta P_a - \Delta\Pi) = \frac{Q_p}{A} \qquad \text{Eq. 1}$$

Where is:

23

F_w = water flux rate, kg/m².s, m/s

k_w = water mass transfer coefficient involving temperature, membrane characteristics, and solute characteristics, s/m, m/s.bar

ΔP_a = average imposed pressure gradient, kg/m.s², bar

$$= \left[\frac{P_f + P_c}{2}\right] - P_p \qquad \text{Eq. 2}$$

$\Delta \Pi$ = osmotic pressure gradient, kg/m.s², bar

$$= \left[\frac{\Pi_f + \Pi_c}{2}\right] - \Pi_p \qquad \text{Eq. 3}$$

Q_p = permeate stream flow, kg/s, m

A = membrane area, m

Some solute passes through the membrane in all cases. Solute flux can be described adequately by an expression of the form:

$$F_i = k_i \,(\Delta C_i) = \frac{Q_p C_p}{A} \qquad \text{Eq. 4}$$

Where is:

F_i = flux of solute species I, kg/m

k_i = solute mass transfer coefficient, m/s

ΔC_i = solute concentration gradient, kg/m³

$$= \left[\frac{C_f + C_c}{2}\right] - C_p \qquad \text{Eq. 5}$$

C_f = solute concentration in feed stream, kg/m³

C_c = solute concentration concentrate stream, kg/m³

C_p = solute concentration permeate stream, kg/m³

The recovery rate and the rate of rejection are as described above for the micro- and ultrafiltration membranes.

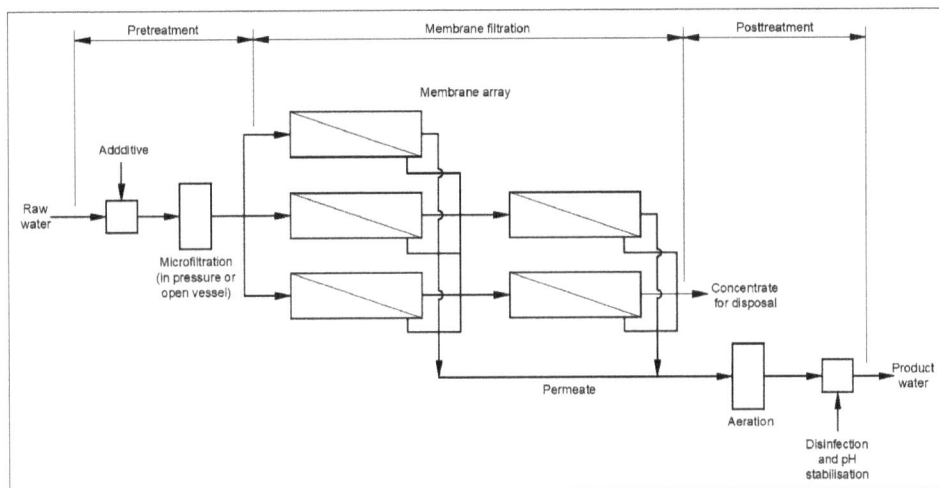

Figure 11: Typical flow diagram for reverse osmosis membrane process with pre- and posttreatment

Membrane fouling

The term *fouling* describes the potential deposition and accumulation of constituents in the feed stream on the membrane. Membrane fouling is an essential consideration in the design and operation of membrane systems as it affects pre-treatment needs. cleaning requirements, operation conditions, cost, and performance. Constituents in water or wastewater that can bring about membrane fouling are identified in Table 2, which can occur in three general forms:

1. A build-up of the constituents in the feedwater on the membrane surface
2. The formation of chemical precipitates due to the chemistry of the feedwater
3. Damage to the membrane is due to the presence of chemical substances that can react with the membrane or biological agents that can colonise the membrane.

Table 2: Constituents in water that can affect the performance of membranes through the mechanism of fouling.

Type of membrane fouling	Responsible constituent	Remarks
Fouling (cake formation, sometimes identified as biofilm formation)	Metal oxides, Organic and inorganic colloids, Bacteria, Microorganisms, Concentration polarisation	Damage to membranes can be limited by controlling these substances (e. g., by use of MF before RO)
Scaling (precipitation)	Calcium sulphate, Calcium carbonate, Calcium fluoride, Barium sulphate, Metal oxide formation, silica	Scaling can be reduced by limiting salt content, by adding acid to limit the formation of calcium carbonate, and by other chemical treatment
Damage to membrane	Acids, Bases, pH extremes, Free chlorine, Bacteria, Free oxygen	Damage to membranes can be limited by controlling these substances. Extent of damage depends on the nature of the membrane

Three accepted mechanisms resulting in resistance to flow due to the accumulation of material within the lumen (see Figure...) are:

(1). pore narrowing,
(2). pore plugging, and
(3). Gel/cake formation caused by the concentration polarisation.

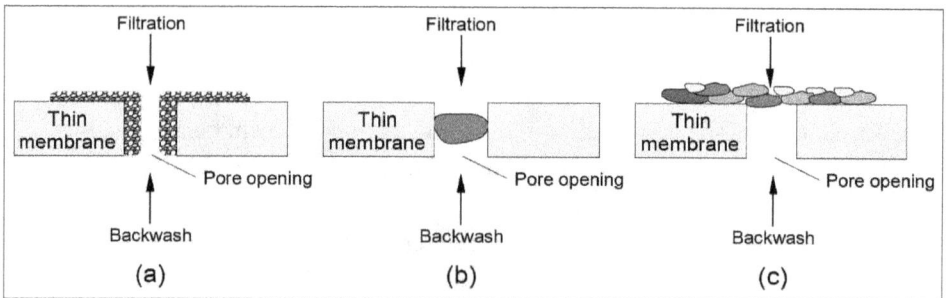

Figure 12: Modes of membrane fouling: (a) pore narrowing, (b) pore plugging, and (c) gel/cake formation caused by concentration polarisation.

Gel/cake formation, caused by concentration polarisation, occurs when most of the solid matter in the feed is larger than the pore size or molecular weight cut-off of

26

the membrane. Concentration polarisation can be described as the build-up of matter close to or on the membrane surface that causes an increase in resistance to solvent transport across the membrane. Some degree of concentration polarisation will always occur in the operation of a membrane system. However, the formation of a gel or cake layer is an extreme case of concentration polarisation where a large amount of matter has accumulated on the membrane surface, forming a gel or cake layer. The pore plugging and pore narrowing mechanism will occur only when the solid matter in the feedwater is smaller than the pore size or the molecular weight cut-off. As the name describes, pore plugging occurs when the particles, the size of the pores become stuck in the membrane's pores. Pore narrowing consists of solid material attached to the interior surface of the pores, which results in a narrowing of the pores. It has been hypothesised that concentration polarisation is amplified further once the pore size is reduced, causing an increase in fouling.

Control of membrane fouling

Typically, three approaches are used to control membrane fouling:

(1). pre-treatment of the feedwater,
(2). membrane backwashing, and
(3). Chemical cleaning of the membranes.

Pre-treatment is used to reduce the TSS and bacterial content of the feedwater. Often the feedwater will be conditioned chemically to limit chemical precipitation within the units. The most used method of eliminating the accumulated material from the membrane surface is backwashing with water and/or air. Chemical treatment is used to remove constituents that are not during the conventional backwashing. Chemical precipitates can be removed by altering the chemistry of the feedwater and by chemical treatment. Damage of the membrane due to deleterious constituents typically cannot be reversed.

Application of membranes

Typical applications of membrane technologies for water and wastewater treatment are shown in

Table *3*. The principal application of various membrane technologies for the removal of specific constituents found in water and wastewater are summarised in Table 4.

Table 3: Typical applications for membrane technologies in water and wastewater treatment

Application	Description
Microfiltration and ultrafiltration	
Aerobic biological treatment	Membrane is used to separate treated wastewater from the active biomass in an activated sludge process. The membrane separation unit can be internally immersed in the bioreactor or external to the bioreactor. Such processes are known as membrane bioreactors (MBR).
Anaerobic biological treatment	Membrane is used to separate the treated wastewater from the active biomass in an anaerobic complete-mixed reactor.
Pre-treatment for effective disinfection	Used to remove residual suspended solids from settled secondary effluent or from the effluent from depth or surface filters to achieve effective disinfection with either chlorine or UV radiation for reuse applications.
Pre-treatment for nanofiltration and reverse osmosis	Microfilters are used to remove residual colloidal and suspended solids as a pre-treatment step for additional processing.
Nanofiltration	
Effluent reuse	Used to treat prefiltered effluent (typically with microfiltration) for indirect potable reuse applications such as groundwater injection. Credit is also given for disinfection when using nanofiltration. Used to reduce the concentration of multivalent ion contributing to hardness for specific reuse applications.
Reverse osmosis	
Effluent reuse	Used to treat prefiltered effluent (typically with microfiltration) for indirect potable reuse application such as groundwater injection. Credit is also given for disinfection when using reverse osmosis.
Effluent dispersal	Reverse osmosis processes have proved capable of removing a sizable number of selected compounds.
Two-stage treatment for boiler use	Two stages of reverse osmosis are used to produce water suitable for high-pressure boilers.

Typical operating ranges in terms of operating pressure and flux rate, along with the types of membranes used, are reported in Table 5.

Table 4: Application of membrane technologies for the removal of specific constituents found in wastewater[a]

Constituent	Membrane technology				Comments
	MF	UF	NF	RO	
Biodegradable organics		✔ -	✔ -	✔ -	
Hardness			✔ -	✔ -	
Heavy metals			✔ -	✔ -	
Nitrate			✔ -	✔ -	
Priority organic pollutants		✔ -	✔ -	✔ -	
Synthetic organic compounds		✔ -	✔ -	✔ -	
TDS			✔ -	✔ -	
TSS	✔ -	✔ -			TSS removed during pre-treatment for NF and RO
Bacteria	✔ - [b]	✔ -	✔ -	✔ -	Used for membrane disinfection. Removed as pre-treatment for NF and RO with MF and UF.
Protozoan cyst and oocysts and helminth ova	✔ -	✔ -	✔ -	✔ -	
Viruses			✔ -	✔ -	Used for membrane disinfection.

[a] specific removal rates will depend on the composition and constituent concentration in the treated water or wastewater

[b] Variable performance

Typical operating ranges in terms of operating pressure and flux rate, along with the types of membranes used, are reported in Table 5.

Table 5: Typical characteristics of membrane technologies used in wastewater-treatment applications.

Membrane technology	Typical operating range	Operating pressure	Rate of flux	Membrane details	
	μm	kPa	L/m².d	Type	Configuration
Microfiltration	0.08-2.0	7-100	405-1600	Polypropylene, acrylonitrile, nylon, polyterafluoro-ethylene	Spiral wound, hollow fibre, plate and frame
Ultrafiltration	0.005-0.2	70-700	405-815	Cellulose acetate, aromatic polyamides	Spiral wound, hollow fibre, plate and frame
Nanofiltration	0.001-0.01	500-1000	200-815	Cellulose acetate, aromatic polyamides	Spiral wound, hollow fibre
Reverse osmosis	0.0001-0.001	850-7000	320-490	Cellulose acetate, aromatic polyamides	Spiral wound, hollow fibre

Typical energy consumption and product recovery values for various membrane systems are presented in Table 6.

Table 6: Typical energy consumption and product recovery values for various membrane systems

Membrane Process	Operation pressure kPa	Energy consumption kWh per m³	Product recovery %
Microfiltration	100	0.4	94-98
Ultrafiltration	525	3.0	70-80
Nanofiltration	875	5.3	80-85
Reverse osmosis	1575	10.2	70-85
Reverse osmosis	2800	18.2	70-85
Electrodialysis		9.5	75-85

2.4 SiC membrane filtration

The application of ceramic membrane technology in water and wastewater is rapidly growing. Inherent advantages of the ceramic membrane, including

30

chemical/thermal stability, low fouling propensity, and long lifespan, make ceramic membrane technology attractive, and the ceramic membrane market is expected to achieve a compound annual growth rate of 12%.

Ceramic membranes could be integrated with advanced oxidation processes such as in-situ ozonation that cannot be applied in the case of the polymeric membrane due to their potential degradation during long-term exposure (Hu et al., 2013).

In addition, the hybrid ceramic membrane processes such as ceramic membrane bioreactor are superior to polymeric counterparts due to higher flux, higher pollutant removal, lower fouling rate and higher cleaning efficiency. Although ceramic membrane has a high capital cost, life-cycle costs of ceramic and polymeric plants are comparable.

Notably, full-scale ceramic membrane water/wastewater treatment plants have been installed in many countries such as Japan, the USA, Singapore, and United Kingdom. Given the attractiveness of this technology, the performance of the ceramic membrane is critically reviewed with a focus on its applications in water and wastewater treatment under mild conditions. In addition, fouling mechanisms and control strategies are elucidated and are compared with polymeric membranes.

Importantly, for the first time, the status of full-scale applications and market prospects of ceramic membranes are critically analysed to show their future potential. Lastly, future research directions such as the development of cost-effective ceramic membranes, understanding the biofouling evolution, and economic evaluation of physicochemical processes for fouling control are proposed.

A CEMBRANE membrane (Cembrane, 2021a) is a unique solid-liquid separation technology based on Silicon Carbide (SiC) ceramic material. It can filter various sources of contaminated water such as suspended solids, bacteria, oil, and heavy metals.

Porosity is one of the most important properties of any membrane technology. High surface porosity means lower membrane fouling rate. Lower fouling rates allow for higher sustainable flux rates. SiC has a surface porosity greater than 50%. Due to such a high surface porosity, SiC can achieve >4 X flux rate than polymeric membranes.

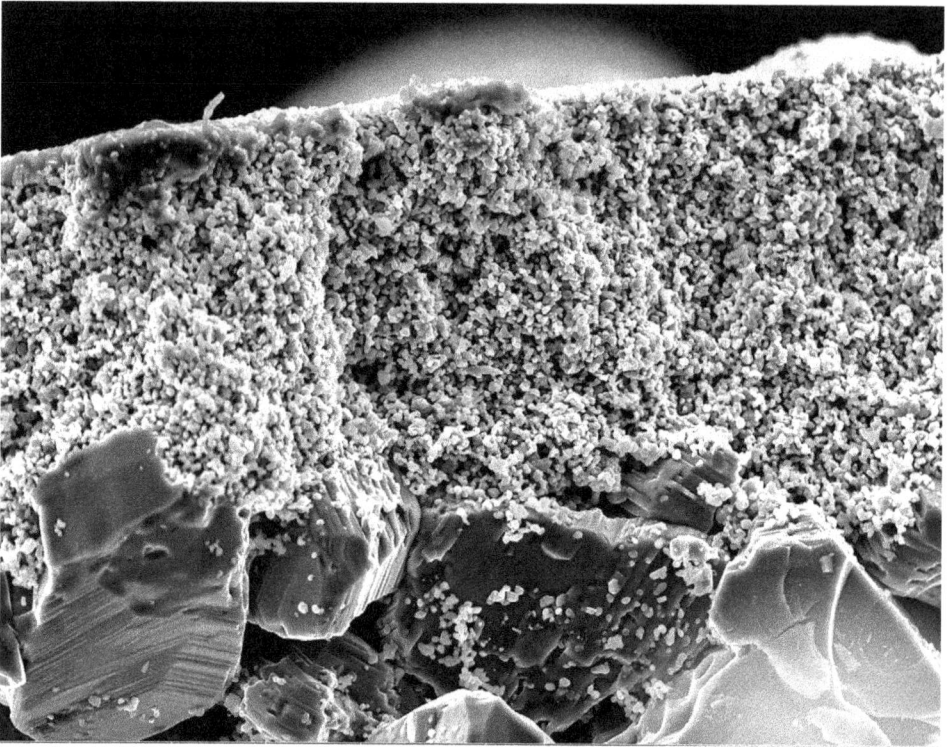

Figure 13: Microscopic image of the SiC membrane (Cembrane, 2021a)

The SiC membrane is made from Silicon Carbide Powder, mixed into a paste, and extruded. The substrate extrusion is fired at 2.200 °C to bond SiC grains. The membrane layer is applied to the substrate. The product is SiC flat plate membrane with 0,1-micron pore size.

The filtration principle is submerged outside, where clean water is drawn through the membrane with suction pressure. Suspended solids and bacteria are rejected on the membrane surface, forming a cake layer while clean water is passing through the membrane body and is collected at both end caps.

The flat sheet membranes are fitted in a square module consisting of 42 individually interchangeable membrane sheets. The module is submersible and can be stacked individually on top of each other, up to 15 modules in total.

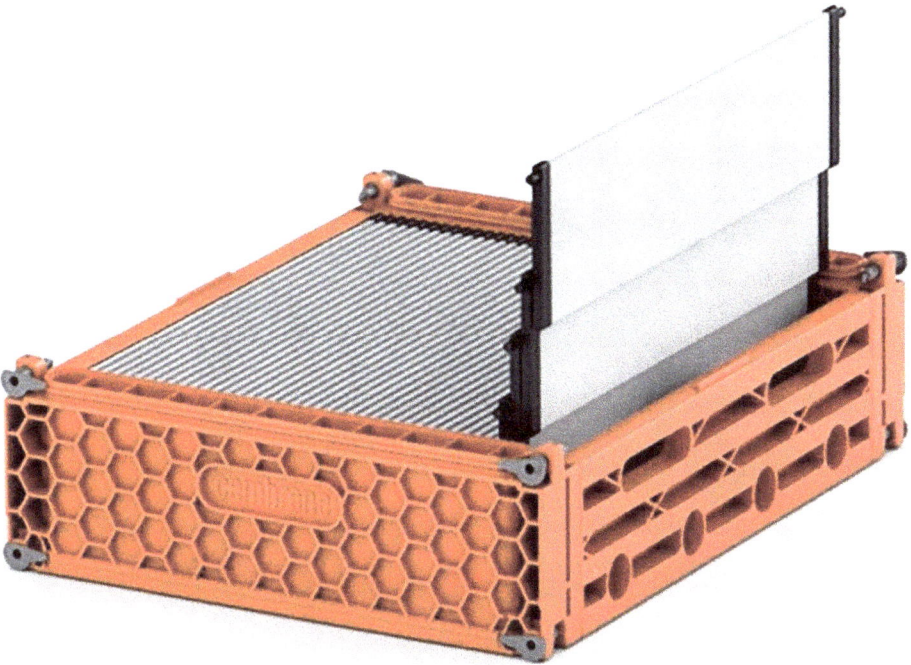

Figure 14: SiC flat sheet membrane and single module (Cembrane, 2021a)

SiC membranes and modules provide some unique advantages in water and wastewater treatment:

- **All in one** process step.
- **High flux rate** reduces footprint, energy, and chemical consumption.
- **Chemically inert** provides high chemical resistance and no permeability decline.
- **Negatively charged** surface reduces the fouling of organics and oil.
- **Extremely hard** and durable makes it easy to clean.
- **High solids loading capability** from few ppm to several % of TSS loading.

Simplified flow sheets combine filtration with sedimentation, flotation, and absorption into one process step.

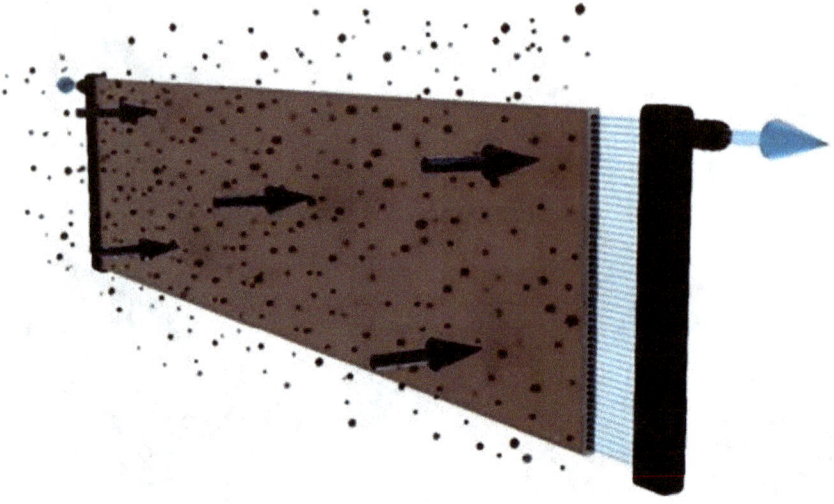

Figure 15: Illustration of outside-in filtration principle on a single membrane sheet (Cembrane, 2021a)

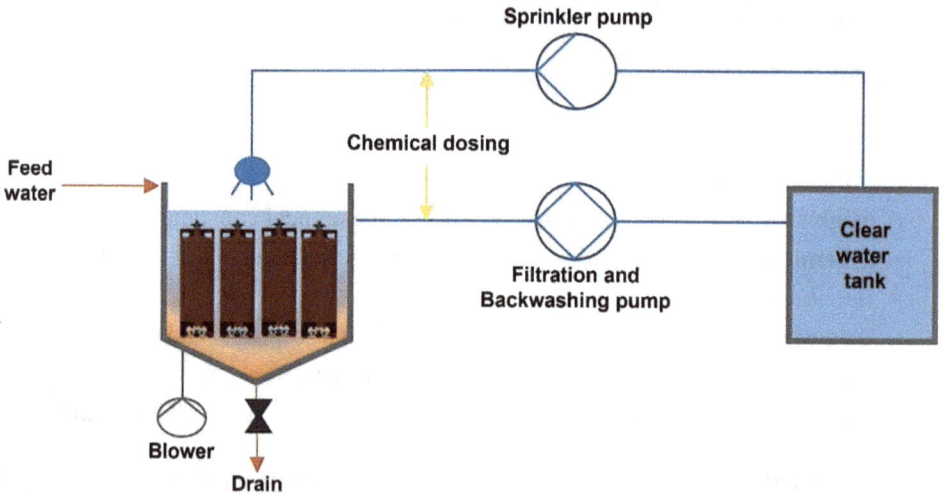

Figure 16: Typical flow chart of SiC membrane process (Cembrane, 2021b).

2.4.1 All in one process step

The process makes the ideal in a wide range of applications. It allows the user to combine several process steps into one.

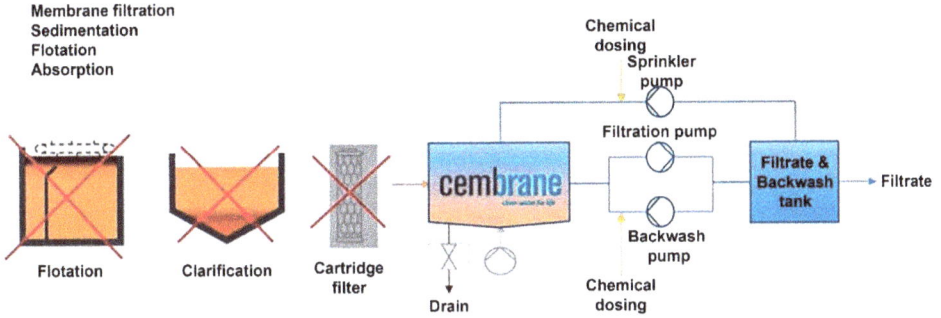

Figure 17: Scheme of the CEMBRANE process (Cembrane, 2021a)

Table 7: Combine filtration with sedimentation, flotation, and absorption into one process step

TANK CONCEPT USING FLAT SHEET SIC MEMBRANE

Permeate ⟶   Feed/influent ⟶   Drain/recirculation ⟶

Tank name	Applications	Benefits	Illustration
Dead-end	• Ground water treatment • Surface water treatment • Sea water • Intake water • Tertiary treatment	• Very slim design • Low footprint • High recovery due to low drainage volume • Almost 100% mass balance can be achieved	
Sedimentration	• Tertiary treatment • Sandfilter & UF backwash water • Mining water • Heavy metal removal • Surface water	• Combination of sedimentation & filtration • Settled solids can be bled off in high solids concentrations (>50%)	
Rolling pattern	• MBR & MBBR • Remineralization of RO effluent • Combination of absorption or reaction & membrane filtration	• High crossflow velocity • Efficient blending using aeration • Filtration combined with **Reaction** tank w. coagulants, minerals, or absorbents such as PAC	
Flow-Through	• MBR • Sludge thickening	• Continuous feed of fresh sludge • High control of TSS reaching membranes • Low risk of dead zones	
Floatration	• Oily wastewater • Produced water • Metal working industry • Food & Beverage	• Combination of DAF with filtration • Treat wastewater with high amount of oil & grease in one step	
In-situ	• MBR • Sludge thickening • Combination of absorption or reaction & membrane filtration	• Use existing tank • Use tank as biology or reaction tank combined with filtration	
Pressurized	• Replacement of cartridge- or bag filters • Treatment of tap water pre-RO • Police filter	• Easy to clean & service • Long life & improved quality water over cartridge filters or bag filters	

2.4.2 High flux rate

The unprecedented high flux rate is mainly due to the high surface porosity and hydrophilic membrane surface.

A membrane´s contact angle to water is an accurate measure of how hydrophilic a membrane is-the more hydrophilic the membrane surface, the higher the operating flux rate.

This results in:

- 3 – 10 x flux compared to polymeric,
- Unmatched low footprint,
- Low-pressure operation at high flow
- High recovery rates,
- Applicable for high sludge concentration.

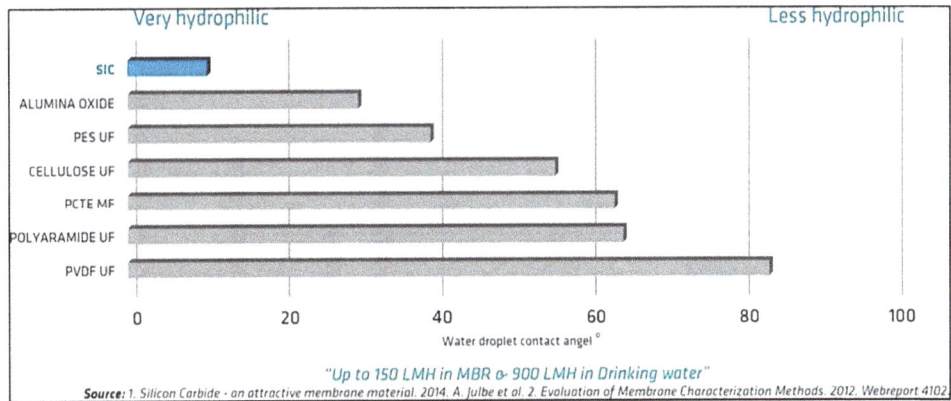

Figure 18: Difference in flux rate between SiC and a polymeric membrane (Cembrane, 2021c)

2.4.3 Chemically inert

The SiC membrane exhibits high chemical resistance. It provides a range of benefits in various applications:

- Can operate in extreme environments,
- Durable and reliable operation,
- Fast and easy restoring of permeability,
- High resistance to wide a pH range, oxidants, even ozone.

37

Table 8: Chemical resistance of SiC and polymeric membrane (Sastri et al., 2007)

Corrosive weight loss (mg/cm²/year)				
Test environment (WT %)	SiC	Al-oxide	Si composite	Tungsten carbide
98% H$_2$SO$_4$; 100°C	1.8	65	55	>1000
50% NaOH; 100°C	2.5	75	>1000	5
25% HCl; 70°C	<0.2	72	0.9	85
45% KOH; 100°C	<0.2	60	>1000	3
70% HNO$_3$; 100°C	<0.2	7	0.5	>1000
85% H$_3$PO$_4$; 100°C	<0.2	>1000	8.8	55
53% HF; 25°C	<0.2	20	7.9	8

2.4.4 Low fouling potential

Due to the negative charge of the membrane surface in the wide pH range, the membrane is less prone to fouling and clogging and allows for more minor maintenance requirements.

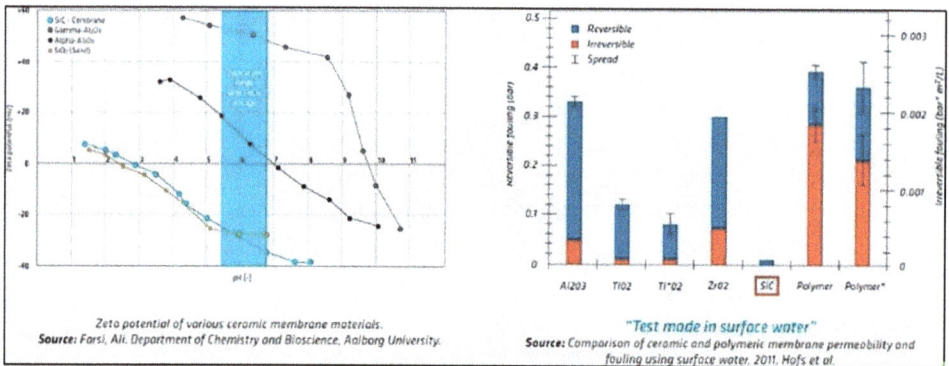

Zeta potential of various ceramic membrane materials.
Source: Farsi, Ali. Department of Chemistry and Bioscience, Aalborg University.

"Test made in surface water"
Source: Comparison of ceramic and polymeric membrane permeability and fouling using surface water. 2011. Hofs et al.

Figure 19: Comparison of SiC and polymeric membrane permeability and fouling rates (Cembrane, 2021b)

This effect is further enhanced by the high surface porosity of the SiC membrane. With a surface porosity of more than 4 x of commonly used membranes, the individual pores experience lower solids loading even at higher flux rates.

2.4.5 Durable and easy to clean

Another critical feature of SiC is the hardness and durability of the membrane material, providing a long life and enabling harsh mechanical cleaning. During a sludge dewatering event, sludge can be trapped between the SiC flat sheet membranes.

However, due to the durability of membranes, sludge can be effectively removed by a pressure washer.

Figure 20: Cleaning SiC membrane with high pressure washer (Cembrane, 2021b)

3 Disinfection

Disinfection refers to the partial destruction of disease-causing organisms. All the organisms are not destroyed during the process. The fact that all the organisms re not destroyed differentiates disinfection from sterilisation, which is the destruction of all organisms. In the field wastewater treatment, the four categories of human enteric organisms of the greatest consequence in producing disease are bacteria, protozoan oocysts and cysts, helminths, and viruses (Tchobanoglous et al., 2003; Ishaq et al., 2019; Saqib et al., 2018).

The purpose of the chapter is to introduce to the general concepts involved in the disinfection of water and wastewater and the design of disinfection systems.

Topics include

(1). disinfection with chloride and related compounds,
(2). disinfection with chlorine dioxide,
(3). disinfection with UV radiation, and
(4). disinfection with ozone.

3.1 Mechanism of disinfectants

The five principal mechanisms that have been proposed to explain the action of disinfectants are:

(1). damage to the cell wall,
(2). alteration of cell permeability,
(3). alteration of the colloidal nature of the protoplasm,
(4). alteration of the organism DNA or RNA, and
(5). inhibition of enzyme activity.

Damage or destruction of the cell wall will result in cell lysis and death. Some agents, such penicillin, inhibit the synthesis of the bacterial cell wall.

Agents such as phenolic compounds and detergents alter the permeability of the cytoplasmic membrane. These substances destroy the selective permeability of the membrane and allow vital nutrients, such as nitrogen and phosphorous to escape.

Heath, radiation, and highly acid or alkaline agents alter the colloidal nature of the protoplasm. Heat will coagulate the cell protein and acids, or bases will denature proteins, producing a lethal effect.

UV radiation can cause the formation of double bonds in microorganism as well as rupturing some DNA strands. When UV photons are absorbed by DNA in bacteria and protozoa and DNA and RNA in viruses, covalent dimers can be formed from adjacent thymine in DNA or uracil in RNA. The formation of double bond disrupts the replication process so that the organism can no longer reproduce and is thus inactivated.

Another mode of disinfection is the inhibition of enzyme activity. Oxidising agents, such as chlorine, can alter the chemical arrangement of enzymes and inactivate the enzymes.

A comparison of the mechanism of disinfection using chlorine, ozone, and UV radiation, commonly used disinfectants for water and wastewater, is shown in Table 9.

Table 9: Mechanisms of disinfection using chlorine, UV, and ozone.

Chlorine	Ozone	UV radiation
1. Oxidation 2. Reaction with available chlorine 3. Protein precipitation 4. Modification of cell wall 5. Hydrolysis and mechanical disruption	1. Direct oxidation/ destruction of cell wall with leakage of cellular constituents outside of the cell 2. Reactions with radical by-products of ozone decomposition 3. Damage to the constituents of the nucleic acids (purines and pyrimidines) 4. Breakage of carbon-nitrogen bonds leading to depolymerisation	1. Photochemical damage to RNA and DNA (e.g., formation of double bonds) within the cells of an organism 2. The nucleic acids in microorganisms are the most important absorbers of the energy of light in the wavelength range of 240-280 nm 3. Because DNA and RNA carry generic information for reproduction, damage of these substances, ca effectively inactivate the cell

3.2 Factors influencing the action of disinfectants

In applying the disinfection agents, the following factors must be considered:

(1). contact time,

(2). concentration of the disinfectant,

(3). intensity and nature of physical agent,

(4). temperature,

(5). type of organisms, and

(6). nature of the suspended liquid.

3.2.1 Contact time

Perhaps one of the most important variables in the disinfection process is contact time. In early 1900s, Harriet Chick observed that for a given concentration of disinfectant, the longer the contact time, the greater the kill. This observation was first reported in the literature in 1908 (Chick, 1908). In the differential form, Chick's law is:

$$\frac{dN_t}{dt} = -kN_t \qquad\qquad \text{Eq. 6}$$

Where:

dN_t/dt = rate of change in the concentration of organisms within time

k = inactivation rate constant, T^{-1}

N_t = number of organisms at time t

t = time

If N_0 is the number of organisms when t in Eq. 6 can be integrated to:

$$\frac{N_t}{N_0} = e^{-kt} \qquad\qquad \text{Eq. 7}$$

or

$$ln\frac{N_t}{N_0} = -kt \qquad\qquad \text{Eq. 8}$$

The value of the inactivation rate k in Eq. 8 can be obtained by plotting $-ln\,(N_t/N_0)$ versus the contact time t.

3.2.2 Concentration of disinfectant

Herbert Watson reported in early 1900s that the inactivation rate constant was related to the concentration as follows (Watson, 1908):

$$k = k'c^n \qquad \text{Eq. 9}$$

Where:

k = inactivation rate constant

k' = die-off constant

n = coefficient of dilution

Combined the expressions proposed by Chick and Watson in differential form yields (Hass and Kara, 1984):

$$\frac{dN_t}{dt} = -k'C^n N_t \qquad \text{Eq. 10}$$

The integrated form of Eq. 10 is:

$$\frac{N_t}{N_0} = e^{-k'C^n t} \qquad \text{Eq. 11}$$

or

$$\ln\frac{N_t}{N_0} = -k'C^n t \qquad \text{Eq. 12}$$

3.2.3 Intensity and nature of a physical agent

Heat and light are physical agents that have been used from time to time in the disinfection of wastewater. It has been found that their effectiveness is a function of intensity. If the decay of organisms can be described with a first-order reaction (Fig. 6), then the effect of the intensity of the physical disinfectant is reflected in the constant k through some functional relationship.

3.2.4 Temperature

The effect of temperature on rate of kill with chemical disinfectants can be represented by a form of the van't Hoff-Arrhenius relationship. Increasing the temperature results in a more rapid kill. In terms of the time t required to effect a given percentage kill, the relationship is:

$$ln\frac{t_1}{t_2} = \frac{E(T_2 - T_1)}{RT_1T_2}$$
Eq. 13

Where is:

t_1, t_2 = time for a given percentage kill at temperatures T_1 and T_2, K, respectively

E = activation energy, J/mole (cal/mole)

R = gas constant, 8.3144 J/mole.K = (1.99 cal/mole.K)

3.2.5 Type of organisms

The effectiveness of various disinfectants will be influenced by the type, nature, and condition of the microorganisms. For example, viable, growing bacteria cells are often killed more easily than older cells that developed a slime coating. In contrast, bacterial spores are extremely resistant, and many of the chemical disinfectants normally used will have little or no effect. Similarly, many of the viruses and protozoa of concern respond differently to each of the chemical disinfectants. In some cases, other disinfecting agents, such as heat or UV radiation, may have to be used. The inactivation of different microorganism groups is considered further in the following sections.

3.2.6 Nature of suspended liquid

In reviewing the development of the various relationships proposed for the inactivation of microorganisms, it is important to note that most of the tests were conducted in batch reactors using distilled or buffered water, under laboratory conditions. In practice, the nature of the suspending liquid must be evaluated carefully. For example, extraneous organic materials will react with most oxidising disinfectants and reduce their effectiveness. The presence of suspended matter will reduce the effectiveness of disinfectants by absorption of the disinfectant and by shielding the entrapped bacteria.

3.3 Disinfection with chlorine

Of all chemical disinfectants, chlorine is the one used most commonly throughout the world. The reason is that chlorine satisfied most of the requirements. Specific topics include a brief description of the various chlorine compounds, a review of chlorine chemistry and breakpoint chlorination, analysis of the performance of chlorine as a disinfectant and the factors that may influence the effectiveness of the chlorination process, a discussion of the formation of disinfection by-products (DBPs), and a consideration of the potential impact of the discharge of DBPs to environment. Disinfection with chlorine dioxide, chlorination and dechlorination, and the design of chlorination facilities are considered in the following sections, respectively.

3.3.1 Characteristics of chlorine compounds

The principal chlorine compounds used at wastewater treatment plants are chlorine (Cl_2), sodium hypochlorite (NaOCl), calcium hypochlorite [$Ca(OCl)_2$], and chlorine dioxide (ClO_2). Many large cities have switched from chlorine gas to sodium hypochlorite because of safety concerns related to handling and storage of liquid chlorine.

3.3.1.1 Chlorine

Chlorine (Cl_2) can be present as a gas or liquid. Chlorine gas is greenish yellow in colour and about 2.48 times as heavy as air. Liquid chlorine is amber coloured and about 1.44 times as heavy as water. Unconfined liquid chlorine vaporises rapidly to gas at standard temperature and pressure with 1 litre of liquid yielding about 450 litres of gas. Chlorine is moderately soluble in water, with a maximum solubility of about 1 percent at 10°C. Chlorine is supplied as a liquified gas under high pressure in containers varying in size from 45 kg and 68 kg cylinders, 908 kg containers, multiunit railcars containing fifteen 908 kg containers, and railcars with capacities of 14.5, 27.3, and 49.9 Mg. Selection of the size of the chlorine pressure vessel depends on an analysis of the rate of chlorine usage, cost of chlorine, facility requirements, and dependability of supply.

Although the use of chlorine for disinfection of both potable water supplies and treated wastewater has been of great significance from a public health perspective, serious concerns have been raised of its continuous use. Important concerns include:

1. Chlorine is a highly toxic substance that is transported by rail and truck, both of which are prone to accidents.
2. Chlorine is a highly toxic substance that potentially poses health risks to treatment plant operators and the general public if released by accident.
3. Because chlorine is a highly toxic substance, stringent requirements for containment and neutralisation must be implemented as specified in the Uniform Fire Code.
4. Chlorine reacts with the organic constituents in wastewater to produce odorous compounds.

45

5. Chlorine reacts with the organic constituents in wastewater to produce by-products, many of which are known to be carcinogenic and/or mutagenic.
6. Residual chlorine in treated wastewater effluent is toxic to aquatic life.
7. Concern exists over the discharge of chloro-organic compounds to the environment whose long-term effects are not known.

3.3.1.2 Sodium hypochlorite

Many of the safety concerns related to the transport, storage, and feeding of the liquid-gaseous chlorine are eliminated using either sodium or calcium hypochlorite. Sodium hypochlorite (NaOCl) (i.e., liquid bleach), is only available as liquid and usually contains 12.5 to 17 percent available chlorine at the time it is manufactured. The solution decomposes more readily at high concentration and is affected by exposure to light and heat. A 16.7 percent solution stored at 26.7 °C will lose 10 percent of its strength in 10 days, 20 percent in 25 days, and 30 percent in 43 days. It must therefore be stored in a cool location in a corrosion-resistant tank. Another disadvantage of sodium hypochlorite is the chemical cost. The purchase price may range from 150 to 200 percent of the cost of liquid chlorine. The handling of sodium hypochlorite requires special design considerations because of its corrosiveness and the presence of chlorine fumes.

3.3.1.3 Calcium hypochlorite

Calcium hypochlorite [$Ca(OCl)_2$] is available commercially in either dry or a wet form. High-test calcium hypochlorite contains at least 70 percent available chlorine. In dry form, it is available as an off-white powder or as granules, compressed tablets, or pellets. Calcium hypochlorite granules or pellets are readily soluble in water, varying from about 21.5 g/100 mL at 0 °C to 23.4 g/100 mL water at 40 °C. Because of its oxidising potential, calcium hypochlorite should be stored in a cool, dry location away from other chemicals in corrosion-resistant containers. With proper storage conditions, the granules are relatively stable. Hypochlorite is more expensive than liquid chlorine, loses its available strength on storage, and may be difficult to handle. Because it trends to crystallise, calcium hypochlorite may clog metering pumps, piping, and valves. Calcium hypochlorite is used most commonly at small installations.

Chlorine reactions in water

When chlorine in the form of Cl_2 gas is added to water, two reactions occur: hydrolysis and ionisation.

Hydrolysis may be defined as the reaction in which chlorine gas combines with water to form hypochlorous acid (HOCl).

$$Cl_2 + H_2O \leftrightarrow HOCl + H^+ + Cl^- \qquad \text{Eq. 14}$$

The equilibrium constant K_H for this reaction is:

$$K_H \frac{[HOCl][H^+][Cl^-]}{[Cl_2]} = 4.5 \times 10^{-4} \ (mole/L)^2 \ at \ 25\,°C \qquad \text{Eq. 15}$$

Because of the magnitude of the equilibrium constant, large quantities of chlorine can be dissolved in water.

Ionisation of hypochlorous acid to hypochlorite ion (OCl⁻) may be defined as:

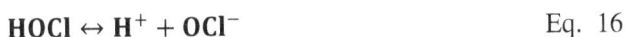

$$HOCl \leftrightarrow H^+ + OCl^- \qquad \text{Eq. 16}$$

The ionisation constant K_i for this reaction is:

$$K_i = \frac{[H^+][OCl^-]}{[HOCl]} = 3 \times 10^{-8} \ mole/L \ at \ 25\,°C \qquad \text{Eq. 17}$$

The variation in the value of K_i with temperature is reported in Table 10.

Table 10: Values of the ionisation constant of hypochlorous acid at different temperatures

Temperature (°C)	$K_i \times 10^8$ (mole/L)
0	1.5
5	1.7
10	2.0
15	2.3
20	2.6
2HOCl+Ca	2.9

The total quantity of HOCl and OCl⁻ present in water is called "free available chlorine". The relative distribution of these two species is essential because the killing efficiency of HOCl is about 40 to 80 times that of OCl⁻. The percentage distribution of HOCl at various temperatures can be computed using Eq. 18.

$$\frac{[\text{HOCl}]}{[\text{HOCl}] + [\text{OCl}^-]} = \frac{1}{1 + [\text{OCl}^-]/[\text{HOCl}]} = \frac{1}{1 + K_i[\text{H}]} = \frac{1}{1 + K_i 10^{\text{pH}}} \qquad \text{Eq. 18}$$

Hypochlorite reactions in water

Free available chlorine can also be added to water in the form of hypochlorite salts. Both calcium and sodium hypochlorite hydrolyse to form hypochlorous acid (HOCl) as follows:

$$\text{Ca(OCl)}_2 + 2\text{H}_2\text{O} \rightarrow 2\text{HOCl} + \text{Ca(OH)}_2 \qquad \text{Eq. 19}$$

$$\text{NaOCl} + 2\text{H}_2\text{O} \rightarrow \text{HOCl} + \text{NaOH} \qquad \text{Eq. 20}$$

Chlorine reactions with ammonia

Untreated wastewater contains nitrogen in the form of ammonia and various organic forms. The effluent from most treatment plants also contains a significant amount of nitrogen, usually in the form of ammonia or nitrate if the plant is designed to achieve nitrification. Because hypochlorous acid is a very active oxidising agent, it will react readily with ammonia in the wastewater to form three types of chloramines in successive reactions:

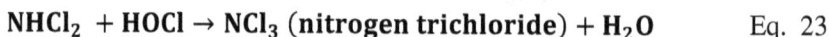

$$\text{NH}_3 + \text{HOCl} \rightarrow \text{NH}_2\text{Cl (monochloramine)} + \text{H}_2\text{O} \qquad \text{Eq. 21}$$

$$\text{NH}_2\text{Cl} + \text{HOCl} \rightarrow \text{NHCl}_2 \text{(dichloramine)} + \text{H}_2\text{O} \qquad \text{Eq. 22}$$

$$\text{NHCl}_2 + \text{HOCl} \rightarrow \text{NCl}_3 \text{ (nitrogen trichloride)} + \text{H}_2\text{O} \qquad \text{Eq. 23}$$

These reactions depend on the pH, temperature, and contact time, and on the ratio of chlorine and ammonia. The two species that predominate, in most cases, are monochloramine (NH_2Cl) and dichloramine ((NHCl_2). The amount of nitrogen trichloride present is negligible up to chlorine-to-nitrogen ratios of 2.0. The chlorine in these compounds is called "combined available chlorine".

Actual and available chlorine

The present actual and available chlorine can be used to compare the effectiveness of compounds containing chlorine. The percent actual chlorine is determined as follows:

48

$$(Cl_2)_{actual}, \% = \frac{\textbf{(weight of chlorine in compound)}}{\textbf{(molecular weight of compound)}} \times \textbf{100} \qquad \text{Eq. 24}$$

Available chlorine is the term used to compare the "oxidising power" of chlorine compounds. The oxidising power of chlorine is based on the value of the valence of the chloride in the compound that is reduced to a valence value of -1. The half reaction for hypochlorous acid is given below:

$$\textbf{HOCl} + \textbf{H}^+ + \textbf{e}^- \rightarrow \textbf{Cl}^- + \textbf{H}_2\textbf{O} \qquad \text{Eq. 25}$$

As shown in Eq. 25, the electron charge is 2. The percent available chlorine is given by the following relationship:

$$\textbf{Cl}_{available} = \textbf{(Cl equivalent)}[(\textbf{Cl}_2)_{actual}, \%] \qquad \text{Eq. 26}$$

For HOCl, the actual percentage of chlorine is 67.7 percent [(35.5/52.5 x 100], and the available chlorine is 135.4 percent (2 x 67.7). Values for the actual and available percent chlorine are given in Table 11 for chlorine and various compounds containing chlorine that have been used as disinfectants.

Table 11: Actual and available chlorine in compounds containing chlorine

Compound	Molecular weight	Chlorine equivalent	Actual chlorine, %	Available chlorine, %
Cl_2	71	1	100	100
Cl_2O	87	2	81.7	163.4
ClO_2	67.5	5	52.5	260
CaClOCl	127	1	56	56
$Ca(OCl)_2$	143	2	49.6	99.2
HOCl	52.5	2	67.7	135.4
$NaClO_2$	90.5	4	39.2	157
NaOCl	74.5	2	47.7	95.4
$NHCl_2$	86	2	82.5	165
NH_2Cl	51.5	2	69	138

Breakpoint reaction with chlorine

The maintenance of a residual (combined or free) for wastewater disinfection is complicated because free chlorine not only reacts with ammonia, as noted previously, but also is a strong oxidising agent. The term "breakpoint chlorination" is the term applied to the process whereby enough chlorine is added to react with all oxidisable

49

substances such that if additional chlorine is added it will remain as free chlorine. The main reason for adding enough chlorine to obtain a free chlorine residual is that effective disinfection can usually then be assured.

3.4 Disinfection with chlorine dioxide

Chlorine dioxide (ClO_2) is another bactericide, equal to or greater than chlorine in disinfecting power. Chlorine dioxide has proved to be an effective virucide, being more effective in achieving inactivation of viruses than chlorine. A possible explanation is that because chlorine dioxide is adsorbed by peptone (a protein), and that viruses have a protein coat adsorption of ClO_2 onto this coating could cause inactivation of the virus. In the past, ClO_2 did not receive much consideration as a wastewater disinfectant due to its high cost.

Characteristics of chlorine dioxide

Chlorine dioxide (ClO_2) is, under atmospheric conditions, a yellow to red unpleasant-smelling, irritating unstable gas with high specific gravity. Because chlorine dioxide is unstable and decomposes rapidly, it is usually generated onsite before its application. Chlorine dioxide is generated by mixing and reacting a chlorine solution in water with a solution of sodium chlorite ($NaClO_2$) according to the following reaction:

$$2NaClO_2 + Cl_2 \rightarrow 2ClO_2 + 2NaCl \qquad \text{Eq. 27}$$

Based on Eq. 27 1.34 mg sodium chlorite reacts with 0.5 mg chlorine to yield 1.0 mg chlorine dioxide. Because technical-grade sodium chlorite is only about 80 percent pure, about 1.68 mg of the technical-grade sodium chlorite would be required to produce 1.0 mg of chlorine dioxide. Sodium chlorite may be purchased and stored as a liquid (generally 25 percent solution) in refrigerated storage facilities.

Chlorine dioxide chemistry

The active disinfecting agent in a chlorine dioxide system is free dissolved chlorine dioxide (ClO_2). At present, the complete chemistry of chlorine dioxide in an aqueous environment is not clearly understood. Because ClO_2 does not hydrolyse in a manner similar to the chlorine compounds. The oxidising power of ClO_2 is often referred to as "equivalent available chlorine". The definition of the term equivalent available chlorine is based on a consideration od the following oxidation half reaction for ClO_2:

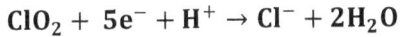

$$ClO_2 + 5e^- + H^+ \rightarrow Cl^- + 2H_2O \qquad \text{Eq. 28}$$

As shown in Eq. 28, the chlorine atom undergoes a 5-electron charge in its conversion from chlorine dioxide to the chloride ion. Because the weight of chlorine in ClO_2 is 52.6 percent and there is a 5-electron charge, the equivalent available chlorine content is equal to 263 percent as compared to chlorine. Thus, ClO_2 is usually expressed in g/m^3. On a molar basis, 1 mole of ClO_2 is equal to 67.45 g, which is equivalent to 177.5 g (5 x 35.45) of chlorine. Thus, 1 g/m^3 of ClO_2 is equivalent to 2.63 g/m^3 of chlorine.

3.5   Ultraviolet radiation (UV) disinfection

The germicidal properties of the radiation emitted from ultraviolet (UV) light sources have been used in a wide variety of applications since its use was pioneered in the early 1900s. With the proper dosage, ultraviolet radiation has proved to be an effective bactericide and virucide for wastewater, while not contributing to the formation of toxic by-products.

Source of UV radiation

The portion of the electromagnetic spectrum in which UV radiation occurs between 100 and 400 nm. The UV radiation range is characterised further according to wavelength as short-wave (UV-A), also known as near-ultraviolet radiation, middle-wave (UV-B), and short-wave (UV-C), also known as UV. The germicidal portion of the UV radiation band is between about 220 and 320 nm, principally in the UV-C range. To produce UV radiation, lamps that contain mercury vapour are charged by striking an electric arc. The energy generated by the excitation of the mercury vapour contained in the lamp results in the emission of UV light. In general, UV disinfection system falls into three categories based on the internal operating parameters of the UV lamp: *low-pressure low-intensity*, *low-pressure high-intensity*, and *medium-pressure high-density* systems. UV disinfection systems may also be classified as open-channel or closed-pipe based on their hydraulic characteristics. In brief, the discussion of UV lamp technology is changing rapidly.

Low-pressure low-density UV lamp

Low-pressure low-density UV lamps generate essential monochromatic radiation at a wavelength of 254 nm, which is close to the 260 nm (255 to 265 nm) wavelength that is considered to be most effective for microbial inactivation. In all cases, mercury-argon lamps are used to generate the IV-C region wavelengths. Low-pressure low-density UV lamps are of s slimline with an overall length of 0.75 to 1.5 m and diameter varying from 15 to 20 mm. These lamps operate optimally at a wall temperature of 40 °C and an internal pressure of 0.007 mm Hg. The output low-pressure low-density lamps are about 25 to 27 W at 254 nm for a power input of 70 to 80 W. Approximately 85 to 88 percent of the lamp output is monochromatic at 254 nm, making it an efficient choice for disinfection processes.

Quartz sleeves are used to isolate the UV lamps from direct water contact and to control the lamp wall temperature by buffering the effluent temperature extremes to which UV lamps are exposed, thereby maintaining a fairly uniform UV lamp output. Because there is an excess of liquid mercury in the low-pressure low-intensity UV lamp, the mercury vapour pressure is controlled by the coolest part of the lamp wall. If the lamp wall does not remain at its optimum temperature of 40 °C, some of the mercury in the lamp condenses back to its liquid state, thereby decreasing the number of mercury atoms available to release photons of UV; hence UV output declines. The output of UV disinfection systems also decreases with time due to a reduction in the electron pool within the UV lamp, deterioration of the electrodes, and the aging of the quartz sleeve. The useful life of a low-pressure low-density UV lamp will vary from 9000 to 13,000 h depending on the number of on-off cycles per day. The useful life of the quartz sleeve is about 4 to 8 years.

Low-pressure high-intensity UV lamp

Low-pressure high-intensity UV lamps are similar to the Low-pressure low-intensity lamps with the exception that a mercury-indium amalgam is used in place mercury. Low-pressure high-intensity UV lamps operate at a higher current discharge and pressure between 0.001- and 0.01-mm Hg. Use of the mercury amalgam allows greater UV-C output, typically from 2 to 4 times the output of conventional low-pressure low-intensity UV lamps. However, one manufacturer offers a lamp that is said to have 20 times the output at 254 nm. The amalgam in the low-pressure high-intensity UV lamps is used to maintain a constant level of mercury atoms, and thus provides greater stability over a broad temperature range and greater lamp life (25 percent greater than other low-pressure lamps).

Medium-pressure high-intensity UV lamp

Medium-pressure high-intensity UV lamps have been developed over last decade. Medium-pressure high-intensity UV lamps, which operate at temperature of 600 to 800 °C and a pressure of 10^2 to 10^4 mm Hg, generate polychromatic radiation. About 27 to 44 percent of the total energy of a medium-pressure high-intensity UV lamp is in the germicidal UV-C wavelength range. Only about 7 to 15 percent of the output is near 254 nm. However, medium-pressure high-intensity UV lamps generate approximately 50 to 100 times the total UV-C output of the conventional low-pressure low-intensity UV lamp. Their use is limited primarily to higher wastewater flows, stormwater overflow, or to space-limited sites because fewer lamps are required, and the footprint of the disinfection system is greatly reduced (i.e. contact time is reduced.

Because high-intensity UV lamps operate at temperatures at which all mercury is vaporised, the UV output can be modulated across a range of the power setting (typically 60 to 100 percent) without significantly charging the spectral distribution of the lamp. The ability to modulate the power is significant with respect to total power usage. Furthermore, because of the high operating temperature, mechanical wiping of the quartz sleeve is essential to avoid the formation of an opaque film on the surface of the sleeve. Although there are a number of manufactures of high-intensity UV lamps, most of the lamp manufacturers do not market complete UV disinfection systems. The particular UV lamp selected by UV system manufacturers is chosen on the basis of an integrated design approach in which the UV lamp, ballast, and reactor design are independent.

3.6 Disinfection with ozone

Ozone was first used to disinfect water supplies in France in the early 1900s. Its use increased and spread into several western European countries and eventually to North America. There are well over 1000 ozone disinfection installations worldwide, almost entirely for treating water supplies. Approximately 200 installations are in operation in North America. A common use for ozone at these installations is for the control of taste-. odour-, and colour producing agents. Although historically used primarily for the disinfection of water, recent advances in ozone are economically more competitive for wastewater disinfection. Ozone can also be used in wastewater treatment for odour control and in advanced wastewater treatment for the removal of soluble refractory organics, in lieu of the carbon adsorption process.

3.6.1 Ozone properties

Ozone is an unstable gas produced when oxygen molecules dissociate into atomic oxygen. Ozone can be produced by electrolysis, photochemical reactions, or radiochemical reaction by electrical discharge. Ozone is often produced by ultraviolet light and lightening during thunderstorm. The electrical discharge method is used for the generation of ozone in water and wastewater disinfection application. Ozone is a blue gas at normal room temperature and has a distinct odour. Ozone can be detected concentration 2×10^{-5} to 1×10^{-4} g/m^3. Because it has an odour, ozone can usually be detected before health concerns develop. The stability of ozone in air is greater than it is in water, but in both cases is on the order of minutes. Gaseous ozone is explosive when the concentration reaches about 240 g/m^3 (20 percent weight in air). The properties of ozone are summarised in Table 12. The solubility of ozone in water is governing by Henry's law. Typical values of Henry's constants for ozone are presented in Table 13.

Table 12: Properties of ozone

Property	Unit	Value
Molecular weight	g	48.0
Boiling point	°C	-111.9 ± 0.3
Melting point	°C	-192.5 ± 0.4
Latent heat of vaporisation at 111.9 °C	kJ/kg	14.90
Liquid density at -183 °C	kg/m^3	1574
Vapour density at 0 °C and 1 atm	g/mL	2.154
Solubility in water at 20.0 °C	mg/L	12.07
Vapour pressure at -183 °C	kPa	11.0
Vapour density compared to dry air at 0 °C and 1 atm	unitless	1.666
Specific volume of vapour at 0 °C and 1 atm	m^3/kg	0.464
Critical temperature	°C	−12.1
Critical pressure	kPa	5532.3

Table 13: Values of Henry's constant for ozone

Temperature, °C	Henry's constant, atm/mole fraction
0	1940
5	2180
10	2480
15	2880
20	3760
25	4570
3	5980

3.6.2 Ozone chemistry

Some of the chemical properties displayed by ozone may be described by its position reactions, which are thought to process as follows:

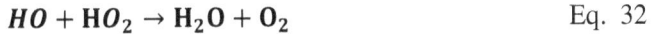

$$O_3 + H_2O \rightarrow HO_3^+ + OH^- \qquad \text{Eq. 29}$$

$$HO_3^+ + OH^- \rightarrow 2H_2O \qquad \text{Eq. 30}$$

$$O_3 + H_2O \rightarrow HO + 2O_2 \qquad \text{Eq. 31}$$

$$HO + HO_2 \rightarrow H_2O + O_2 \qquad \text{Eq. 32}$$

The free radicals formed, HO_2 and HO, have great oxidising powers, and are probably the active form in the disinfection process. These free radicals also possess the oxidizing power to react with other impurities in aqueous solutions.

3.6.3 Energy requirements

The major requirement for power is the conversion of oxygen in ozone. Additional power is required for the preparation of the feed gas, contacting the ozone., destroying the residual ozone, and for the control, instrumentation, and monitoring facilities. The energy requirements for the major components are reported in Table 14.

Table 14: Typical energy requirements for the application of ozone

Component	kWh/kg ozone
Air preparation (compressor and dryers)	4.4–6.6
Ozone generation: - Air feed - Pure oxygen	 - 13.2–19.8 - 6.6–13.2
Ozone contacting	2.2–6.6
All other uses	1.2–2.2

3.6.4 Preparation of feed gas

Ozone can be generated using air, oxygen-enriched air, or high-purity oxygen. If air is used for ozone generation, it must be conditioned by removing the moisture and particulate matter before being introduced into the ozone generator. The following steps are involved in conditioning the air: (1) gas compression, (2) air cooling and drying, and (3) air filtration. If high-purity oxygen is used, the conditioning steps are not required.

3.6.5 Ozone generation

Because ozone is chemically unusable, it decomposes to oxygen very rapidly after generation, and thus must be generated onsite. The most efficient method of producing ozone today is by electrical discharge. Ozone is generated from either air or high-purity oxygen when a high voltage is applied across the gap of narrowly spaced electrodes (see Figure 21: Schematic detail of the generation of ozone). The high-energy corona created by this arrangement dissociates one oxygen molecule, which re-forms with two other oxygen molecules to create two ozone molecules. The gas stream generated by this process from air will contain about 1 to 3 percent ozone by weight, and from pure oxygen about three times that amount, or about 3 to 10 percent ozone in the latest ozone generators.

Figure 21: Schematic detail of the generation of ozone

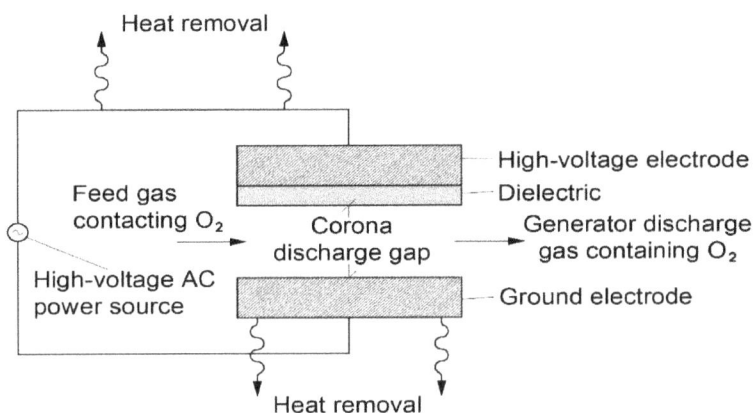

3.6.6 Effectiveness of ozone as a disinfectant

Ozone is an extremely reactive oxidant, and it is generally believed that bacterial kill through ozonation occurs directly because of cell wall disintegration (cell lysis). The impact of the wastewater characteristics on ozone disinfection is reported in Table 15.

Table 15: Impact of wastewater constituents on the use of ozone for wastewater disinfection

Constituent	Effect
BOD, COD, TOC etc.	Organic compounds that comprise BOD and COD can exert on ozone demand. The degree of interference depends on their functional groups and their chemical structure.
Humic materials	Affect the rate of ozone decomposition and the ozone demand
Oil and grease	Can exert on ozone demand
TSS	Increase ozone demand and shielding of embedded bacteria
Alkalinity	No or minor effect
Hardness	No or minor effect
Ammonia	No or minor effect, can react at high pH
Nitrite	Oxidised by ozone
Nitrate	Can reduce effectiveness of ozone
Iron	Oxidised by ozone
Manganese	Oxidised by ozone
pH	Affects the role of ozone decomposition
Industrial discharges	Depending on the constitution may lead to diurnal and seasonal variations in the ozone demand

Ozone is also a very effective viricide and is generally believed to be more effective than chloride. Ozonation does not produce dissolved solids and is not affected by the ammonium ion or pH influent to the process. For these reasons, ozone is considered as an alternative to either chlorination or hypo chlorination, especially where dichlorination may be required and high-purity oxygen facilities are available at the treatment plant.

4 Microplastics

Microplastics are tiny plastic particles up to 5 mm in diameter. In the last four decades, concentrations of these particles appear to have increased significantly in the wastewater, drinking water, and in surface waters of the ocean (UNEP, 2021).

The emission of microplastics into nature poses a threat to aquatic and terrestrial ecosystems. Their penetration of the food chain presents a danger to human health as well. Wastewater treatment plants can be seen as the last barrier between microplastics and the environment. This review focuses on the impact of waste treatment plants in retaining microplastics. Studies show that no wastewater treatment method leads to a complete retention of microplastics, and so wastewater treatment plants themselves are viewed as point sources for the discharge of microplastics into the aquatic environment. Problems associated with the utilization of microplastic loaded sewage sludge are also discussed in the review (Habib et al., 2020).

Microplastics have recently been detected in drinking water as well as in drinking water sources (Koelmans et al., 2019).

Microplastic is an emerging global pollutant that have attracted a great deal of attention from researchers and the public (Li et al., 2021).

The presence of nano and microplastics in water has increasingly become a major environmental challenge. (Enfrin, Dumee, & Lee, 2019).

Conventional wastewater treatment with primary and secondary treatment processes efficiently removes microplastics (MPs) from the wastewater. Despite the efficient removal, final effluents can act as entrance route of MPs, given the large volumes constantly discharged into the aquatic environments. Microplastics (MPs) are defined as plastic particles < 5 mm.

Primary MPs are intentionally manufactured in small sizes like virgin resin pellets, microbeads in personal care products, industrial scrubbers used in abrasive cleaning agents and plastic powders used for moulding, while secondary microplastics result from the fragmentation of larger plastic particles. Fragmentation can occur during the use of materials like textiles, paint and tyres, or once the plastics have been released into the environment. (Talvitie et al., 2017).

5 Membrane filtration and ozonation system

5.1 Development of MFO pilot plant for wastewater treatment

Our first step was to assemble a membrane filter with an ozone generator (MFO) that would be easy to use and require minimum filtration pressure (Rihter Pikl et al., 2021). We constructed a pilot plant for membrane filtration with additional ozonation. The MFO pilot plant consists of the following parts (): 1.) Reservoir 1 (R1), 2.) Filter (F1 and F2), 3.) Reservoir 2 (R), 4.) Microfilter (MF), 5.) Control panel, 6.) two pumps (P1 and P2), power 30 W (15 V, 1.6-2.5 A), 7.) Diaphragm pump (2.4 bar), 8.) Valves (V1, V2, V3, V4) and corresponding connections.

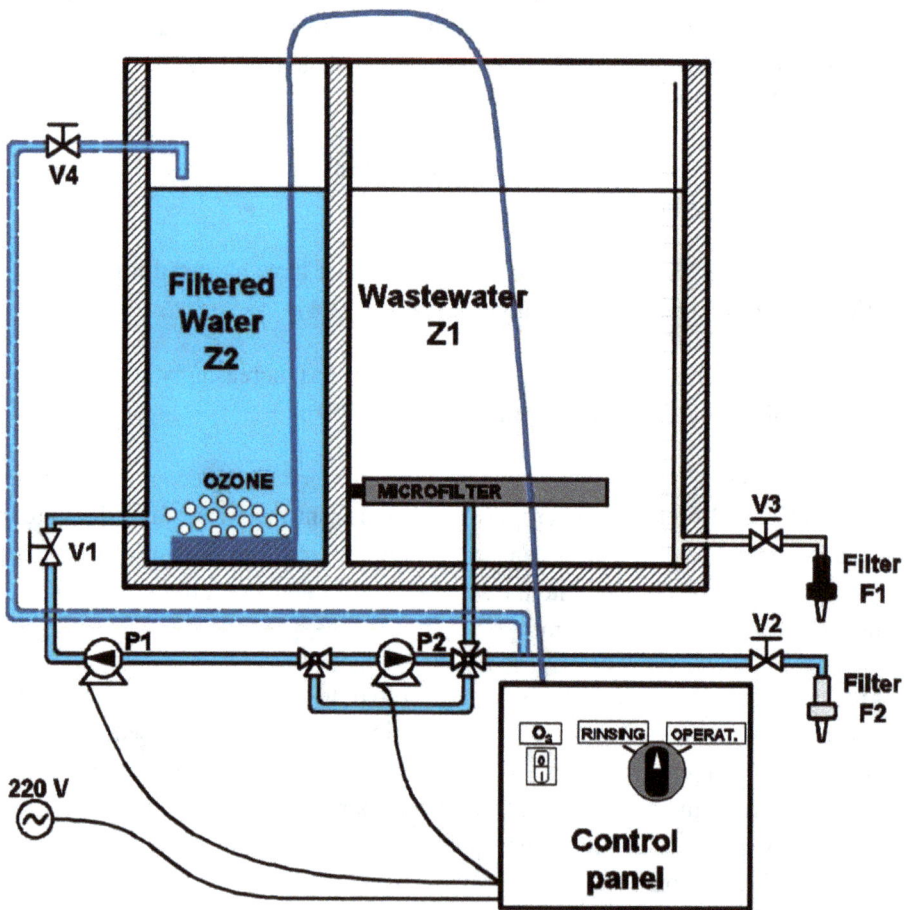

Figure 22: Scheme of the MFO

We prepared 20 L of treated water (effluent) and analysed samples before and after filtration on the parameters: chemical oxygen demand (COD), biochemical oxygen demand (BOD$_5$), ammonium nitrogern (NH$_4$–N), total nitrogen (N$_{total}$), total phosphorous (P$_{total}$), suspended solids (TSS) and microbiological analysis of water - coliform bacteria and *E. coli*. A certain amount of water flowing out of WWTP was poured into reservoir 1 (R1), in which a microfilter made of silicon carbide (SiC) with pores of 100 nm, manufactured by CEMBRANE (Denmark), and constructed by TF LAB d.o.o. The active area of the microfilter is 462 cm^2. The purpose of MF is to retain suspended solids more significant than 100 nm (activated sludge residues, microfibres, and bacteria). A microfibre sampling filter is installed behind the V3 valve. For microfibre analysis (size 300 nano-bubbles up to 5 mm), take a certain amount of water sample from R1 and drain some of the water through the filter by inserting a filter cloth (e.g., feel of a specific gradation) into the device, open the valve (V3) and filter a certain amount of water. From R1, the water is pumped (filtered) into tank 2 (R2), volume 8 L, where the filtered water flowing through the microfilter is collected. The control panel is multipurpose. It contains a) ozone generator, b) a switch for pump drive 1 (P1), and c) a switch for pump drive 2 (P2). From the control panel, the pipe leads to tank R2, through which ozone is conducted. At the bottom of R2 is a ceramic diffuser. The exact time required for microfiltration of a certain amount of water from R1 to R2 was measured. The process of water passage through the membrane took 3.5 min / 5 L of water. After treating filtered water and taking samples for microscopic analysis, the ozone generator was turned on for 2 minutes. 107 mg of O$_3$ was used for 8 L of filtered water ozonated for 2 minutes. We performed the same analyses as before, including microbiological analysis (coliform bacteria, E. coli).

Complete operation conditions of MFO system were:

- complete surface of the SiC filter: 462 cm^2 = 0.0462 m^2
- filter pore size: 100 nm
- flow rate through filter: 0.6 min/L = 21.645 L/h = 21,645 m^3/h
- flowrate through filter: 0.6 min/L = 21,645 L/h = 21.645 m^3/h
- ozonation: 13.4 mg O$_3$/L = 13.4 g/m^3
- filter lifetime: 20 years.

6 Application of SiC membrane filtration

6.1 Drinking water treatment

SiC ceramic membrane modules enable a durable, reliable, and cost-effective treatment to remove heavy metals, TSS and turbidity, organics, silt, bacteria, dissolved organics and algae, whether for RO pre-treatment or direct drinking water consumption (Cembrane, 2021b)

6.2 Industrial Wastewater Reuse

Key benefits in industrial water are high chemical tolerance, high solid loading tolerance and high flux rate.

SiC membrane is widely applied in many industrial water treatment applications. For example, as pretreatment with reverse osmosis or nanofiltration. Using the new generation of the ceramic membrane will enable durable maintenance and a working life expected to exceed 20 years. Moreover, it enables filtration fluids where organic and other ceramic membranes fall short, such as high or low pH, solvents, polymers, and oxidants.

The durability is manifested in a low fouling tendency with extended backwash frequencies and the ability to withstand periodic high sludge loading up to 50.000 ppm without clogging. The membrane can always be regenerated because it enables high-pressure backwash, high-pressure cleaning and back pulse, and a chemical resistance permitting cleaning with harsh chemicals. Additionally, the membranes have one of the highest flux rates for any membrane material, which give an exceptionally low packing density and thereby limited tank footprint.

Unique benefits in MBR:

- Ideal solutions for containerized and modular applications,
- High chemical resistance, tolerate ozone backwashing,
- No fibre breakage,
- Can be stored dry or wet,
- Can always be regenerated,
- Low fouling potentials prolong the filtration cycle and reduce risk of fouling,
- Simple add-on of membrane modules to increase capacity,
- Durable and robust.

6.3 SiC Membrane projects

6.3.1 Hydro recycler – Recycle and Reuse the wash water from the boat pressure washer

Wastewater that drains to surface waters is considered an illegal discharge under the federal Clean Water Act. Even small amounts of untreated pressure washing wastewater can adversely impact water quality and accumulate in bottom sediments. Toxic residues from anti-fouling bottom paints can result in future problems and expenses for marina operators when faced with dredging contaminated sediments and their disposal.

The clean marina program is a partnership of private marina owners, government marina operators and yacht clubs. It was developed to provide clean facilities to the boating community and protect waterways from pollution.

Pressure-washing wastewater includes dirt, algae, barnacles, salts, and paint particles. These small paint particles are the source of heavy metals. About 90% of the heavy metals; copper, lead, tin, zinc, and arsenic, are solid particles that are not dissolved.

Typical untreated pressure-washing wastewater samples contain copper levels in the 50 to 190 mg/l range, while typical municipal sewer standards limit copper concentrations to the 2.4 to 8 mg/L range. The allowed copper concentration in waterways is only 0.006 mg/l, making even treated wash water discharges virtually impossible.

PROBLEM 1: Boat owners enjoy their time on the boats while sailing, but … on the part of the vessel, submerged below the sea level, various organisms such as algae, shells and other sea creatures are accumulating and populating the bottom of the hull. Vessels are therefore significantly reducing their navigability and even increased fuel consumption. It causes additional maintenance requirements and involves extra expenses for boat owners.

SOLUTION: anti-vegetative paint or anti-fouling the boat is painted once a year with anti-fouling paint. Paint layers protect the vessel from uncontrolled exploration of the sea organisms. The applied paint layer contains biocidal products, which will not allow the development of microorganisms on board.

PROBLEM 2: While doing annual boat maintenance, a new layer of Anti-fouling paint must be applied. However, before applying the new paint, the old paint must be removed with a high-pressure power washer. Old paint Layers are decanted and run off into oil trappers when the larger particles stop, while small particles and washing water full of heavy metals and other biocides are freely fused into the sea.

SOLUTION: HYDRO RECYCLER

We collect the wastewater, put it through the filtration system to clean it up, and reuse it. We can do this repeatedly, and by doing this:

- we do not pollute the environment with toxic wastewater.
- We save water, as we repeatedly use the same water for the process.
- we do not have any problems during the dry period and in the time of drinking water reductions.
- We use clean water that does not leave any stains on the boat.
- zero-waste concept.

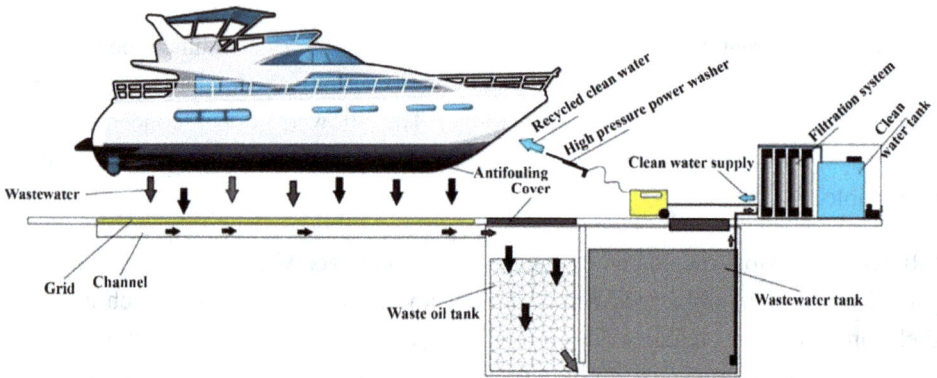

Figure 23: Recycling and reusing wastewater from high pressure power washer

6.3.2 Zero microfibre discharge

Stopping pollution with microplastic fibres from industrial washing machines

He wastewater from the washing machine enters the central reservoir. This water is full of microfibres with different dimensions and weights. At the bottom of the container are placed the membranes. The pump pumps the water through the membrane with the pore size 0.10 microns. The purified water is free of microfibres and is and is ready to be drained. Part of the purified water is stored in the container, and when needed, the backwash pump uses this water for cleaning the membranes. In the process of membrane, a small cleaning amount of ozone is added into the water for membrane disinfection. Pump 3 pushes the wastewater and the concentrate through the filter bag. The filter bag catches and dries the microfibres. When the bag is complete, it should be replaced with a new one. The entire bag is ready to be recycled.

The process is fully automatic and is run by the controller. The whole system does not need any chemical compounds for working.

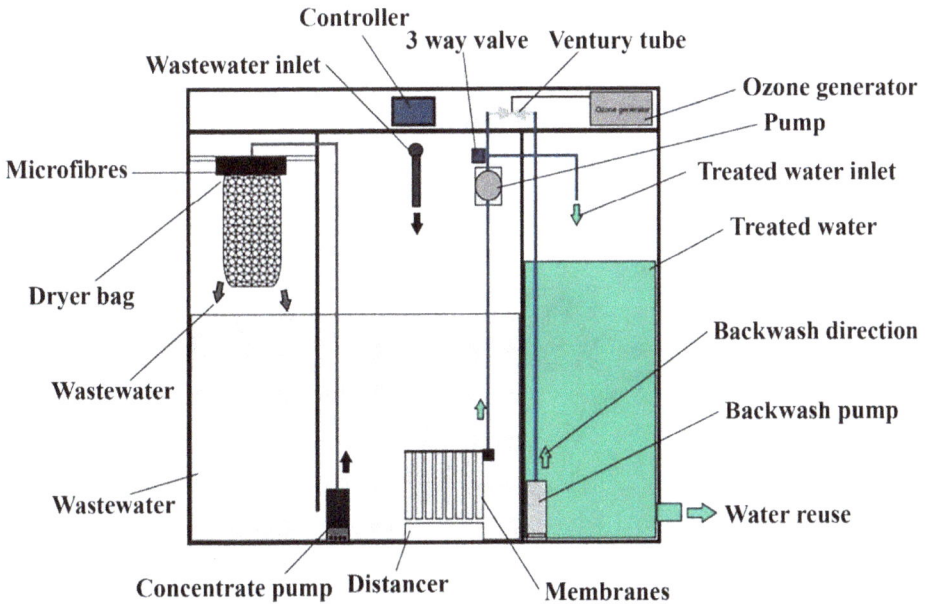

Figure 24: Recycling and reusing wastewater from industrial washing machine

6.3.3 Aquasolar

Solving the problem of drinking water on the field

In nature, there are microorganisms that are life-threatening for humans. Since they cannot be seen with the naked eye, they cannot be avoided.

Aquasolar is the solution where drinking water is a problem. With the right combination of various water treatment technologies Aquasolar provides pure drinking water in emergency situations. This is the solution for humanitarian aid, response to natural disasters, military operations, remote communities, remote industry & research, emergency preparedness.

The combination of Sic membrane, ozone generator, multimedia filters, nano filters, and reverse osmosis membranes allows to physically remove pathogens, particulates, and chemical contaminants from virtually any water source including rivers, lakes, streams, ponds, shallow wells, springs, and sea water. The system provides high quality drinking water in a second without the use of chemicals. Utilizes solar energy and an automated self – cleaning membrane system and it can be used in remote locations anywhere around the world.

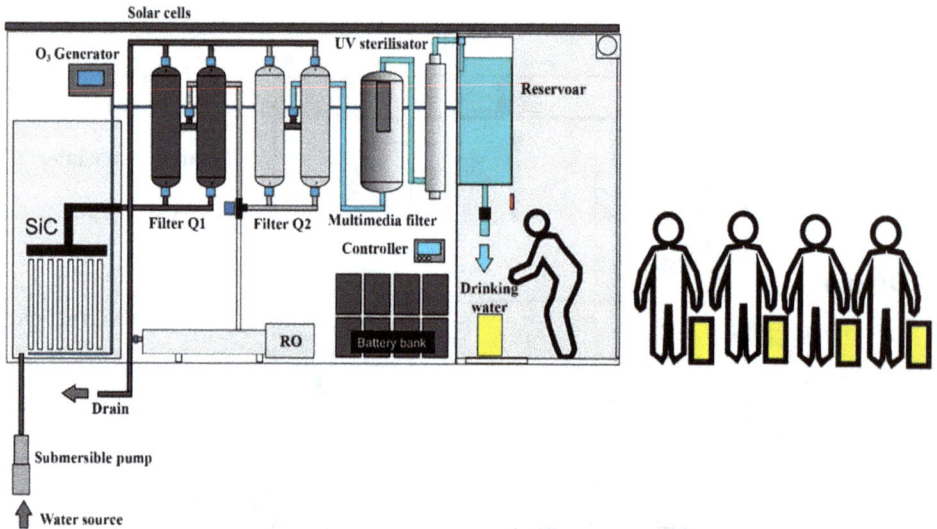

Figure 25: Providing pure drinking water in emergency situations

6.3.4 AquaPillar

Mobile Water Purification System

Aquapillar mobile water purification system is built to work in remote areas and extreme conditions. The system provides high quality drinking water in a second without use of chemicals. Aquapillar physically removes pathogens, particulates, and turbidity from virtually any water source, including rivers, lakes, streams, ponds, shallow wells, and springs.

By using only electric energy from batteries Aquapillar can produce up to 2000 litres of drinking water from microbiologically and chemically affected water sources in one hour.

In emergency situations it can satisfy the daily needs of drinking water for more than 10.000 people.

Technology

AquaPillar uses the patented multimedia smart filter system. This combination of multiple media differing hydrodynamic mechanical properties quickly and effectively eliminates dangerous substances without creating additional mechanical loads.

Aquapillar include a built-in nanofilter, consisting of thermally bonded microglass and cellulose fibres interlaced with nano-alumina fibres in a non –woven matrix that creates a deep electropositive charge in the filter medium, this guaranty a unique combination of effectiveness, capacity and speed of filtration while meaning low mechanical losses.

AquaPillar consists of a low voltage ozone generator, purposely developed for this application. The ozone generator, together with the silicon carbide membrane is incorporated into the integrated system. This combination allows a continuous self-cleaning and disinfection of the system.

Figure 26: AquaPillar at work

Raw water

Drain

 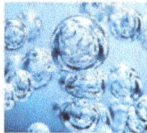 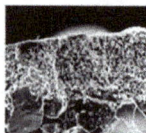  

MEMBRANE   OZONE   MEMBRANE   MULTIMEDIA   NANO

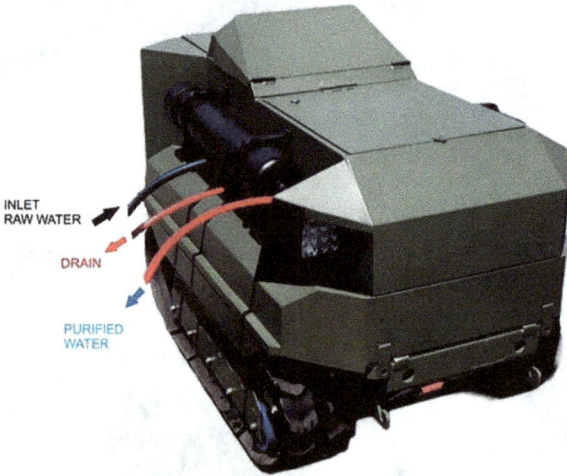

INLET
RAW WATER

DRAIN

PURIFIED
WATER

DRINKING WATER

Figure 27: AquaPillar system

6.3.5 Microplastics problems and microplastics detection

Plastic was invented in 1907. It brought significant improvements to our society and economy. The plastic invention had offered a new source without being limited from natural sources. However, 100 years later, plastic became a huge environmental pollution problem (Braun et al., 2018; Cowger et al., 2019).

Microplastic fibres

Next to obvious plastic pollution caused by plastic bottles, bags, and non-re-use plastic products, many tiny invisible microplastic fibres are deriving from synthetic clothing.

When the fleece is washed, hundreds of tiny polyester fibres are released. The fibres are too small to be caught by washing machine filters and flow into the sewage system, ending up in the sea. Fish mistake these fibres for food, putting them at risk of suffocation. They could even cause damage to humans if they are eaten by tuna, crabs or other creatures that end up in the supermarket.

We are filling our oceans with microplastic approximately 8000 tons of primary microplastics are generated annually in Norway. About half will end up in the ocean.

Microplastic fibres in tap water

Microscopic plastic fibres and fragments are found in drinking water worldwide (Koelmans et al., 2019).

Worldwide, 83% of water samples contain microplastic, in Europe 72% and USA 94%.

Microplastic could be detected ONLY visually by the microscope. It means a certain quantity of sample water is needed to detect a microfibre. Counting fibres show how polluted the sample water is.

Slovenian company TF Lab developed a microplastic detection system allowing microfibres detection per litre on the field, possibility of microscope photos saving on USB, sending results directly to the laboratory. Microplastic is captured in the concentrator disc. Concentrator disc allows selection of fibres material with IR system and possibility of microfibres counting.

Figure 28: Microplastic Detection System

Figure 29: Concentration Head

Figure 30: Concentration Disk

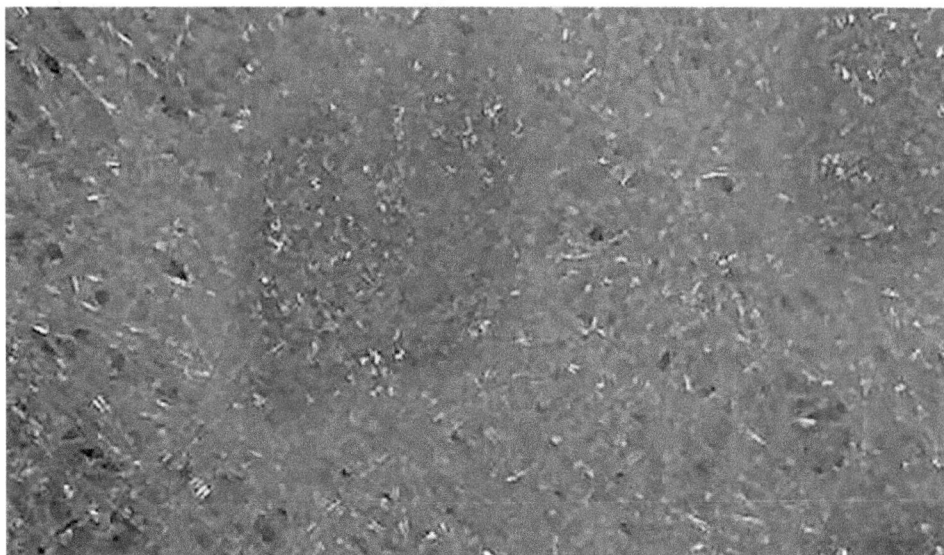

Figure 31: Filter before detection of microfibres and microplastic debris

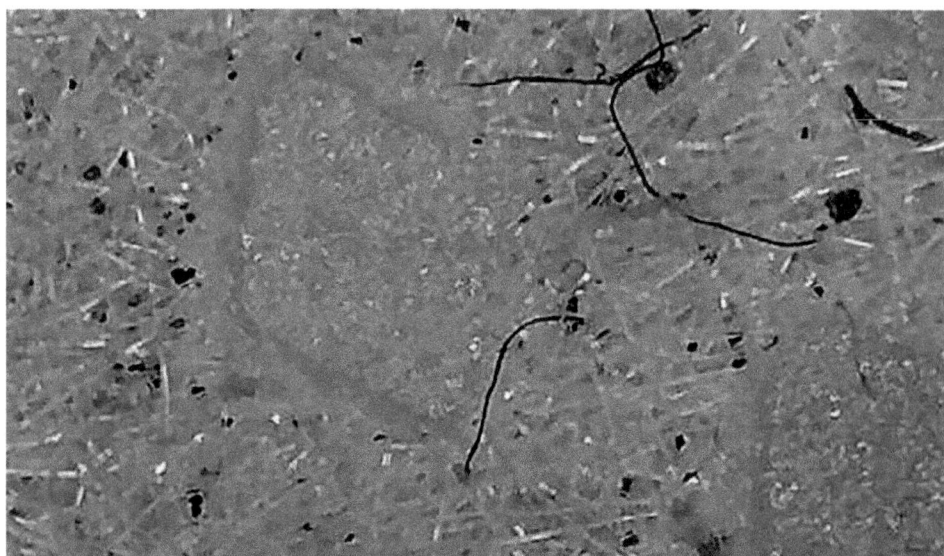

Figure 32: Detected microfibres and microplastic debris

7   Municipal wastewater treatment with membrane filtration and ozonation

Experiments are based on modern wastewater treatment with a combination of conventional municipal wastewater treatment and additional treatment with a membrane filter (SiC membrane with pores of 100 nm) and ozone (O_3). With this type of treatment, it is possible to remove residual contaminants, which cannot be achieved in a conventional treatment plant. A hybrid filter device with an ozone generator (MFO system) has proven to be effective in removing solid and partially colloidal particles, and with parallel ozonation, wastewater can be treated with bacteriological integrity (Mendret et al., 2019; Wang et al., 2021).

The tests were performed at the Shalek Valley Central Wastewater Treatment Plant (WWTP), which has a capacity of 50,000 population equivalents (PE). It works by the process of biofiltration with fixed biomass and treats about 15,000 m^3/day of wastewater. In 2020, 5,685,512 m^3 of wastewater was treated at the WWTP. After biological treatment (primary, secondary, and tertiary steps), the water flows into a nearby watercourse. Wastewater flowing to the biological stage (inflow) and already treated water (effluent) flowing from the WWTP into the natural aquatic environment were used for sampling. Water sampling was performed as a capture of the current sample. Analyses were performed on the concentrations of organic substances (chemical oxygen demand - COD and biochemical oxygen demand - BOD_5), total suspended solids (TSS), including microplastics, and nitrogen (N) and phosphorus (P) compounds. After disinfection with effluent O_3 and filtered water, tests for the presence of common coliform bacteria and *Escherichia coli* were performed.

The definition of the terms given in the tests is as follows: Influent - wastewater flowing to the treatment plant, Effluent - treated wastewater flowing from the treatment plant, Filtered water- wastewater (influent/effluent) passing through the membrane and ozonated water - water that passes through the membrane and is additionally treated with ozone (Rihter Pikl et al., 2021).

7.1   COD removal from influent and effluent using the MFO system

Chemical oxygen demand (COD) is a parameter that tells the amount of oxygen needed for the chemical oxidation of organic pollution in wastewater and represents the mass concentration of oxygen equivalent to the amount of dichromate consumed under certain conditions (Roš & Zupančič, 2010). The average annual value of COD at the Shalek Valley WWTP at the inflow is 225 mg/L. From the figure (Figure 33), a slight fluctuation of the COD value in the inflow is detected due to the different inflow of water. At the time of the measurements, the COD values ranged from 95.9 mg/L to 127 mg/L, which means the average load of raw wastewater. After microfiltration, the COD values decreased from 27 mg/L to 33.2 mg/L, which means that a 76% cleansing effect was achieved. The European Urban Waste Water Treatment Directive (EU Directive 91/271/EEC) sets the limit values for the concentration of COD in the effluent at 110 mg/L. The results show that, given the decrease in the COD value, less polluted water could be purified by microfiltration, as the achieved values are much lower than prescribed.

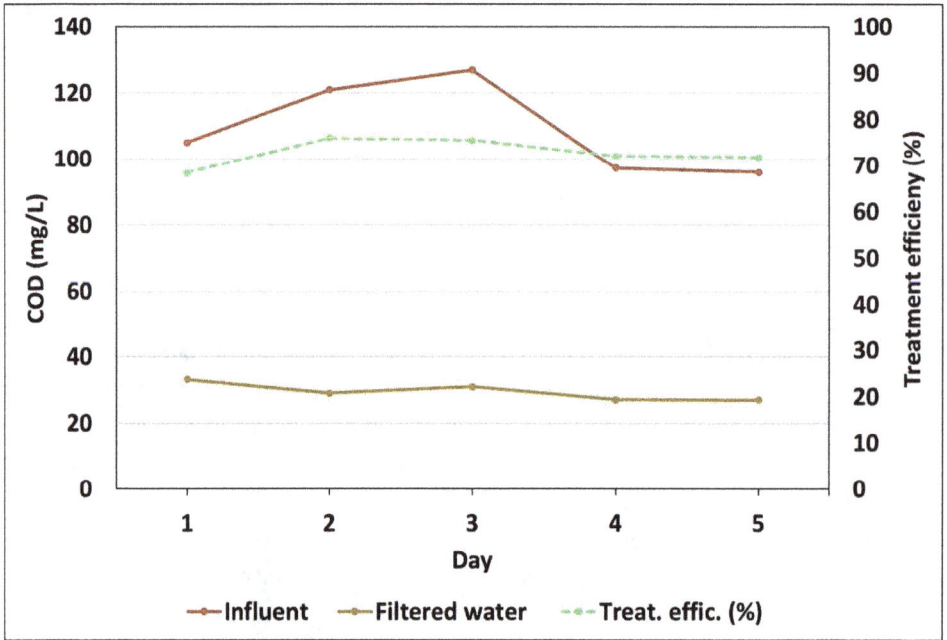

Figure 33: COD of the influent and removal efficiency after microfiltration

7.2 COD removal from effluent using the MFO system

The average annual COD value at the Shalek Valley WWTP at the outflow is 25 mg/L. The figure (Figure 34) shows the COD values in the effluent before microfiltration, which ranged from 28.8 mg/L to 51 mg/L. After microfiltration, COD values decreased from 15.8 mg/L to 23.7 mg/L. It means that a cleaning effect of up to 55.9% was achieved. Compared to the inflow (Figure 33), microfiltration further purified an additional 50% of the COD in the effluent, meaning that the membrane retained much organic matter. The European Urban Wastewater Treatment Directive sets the limit values for the concentration of COD in the effluent at 110 mg/L (Roš & Zupančič, 2010).

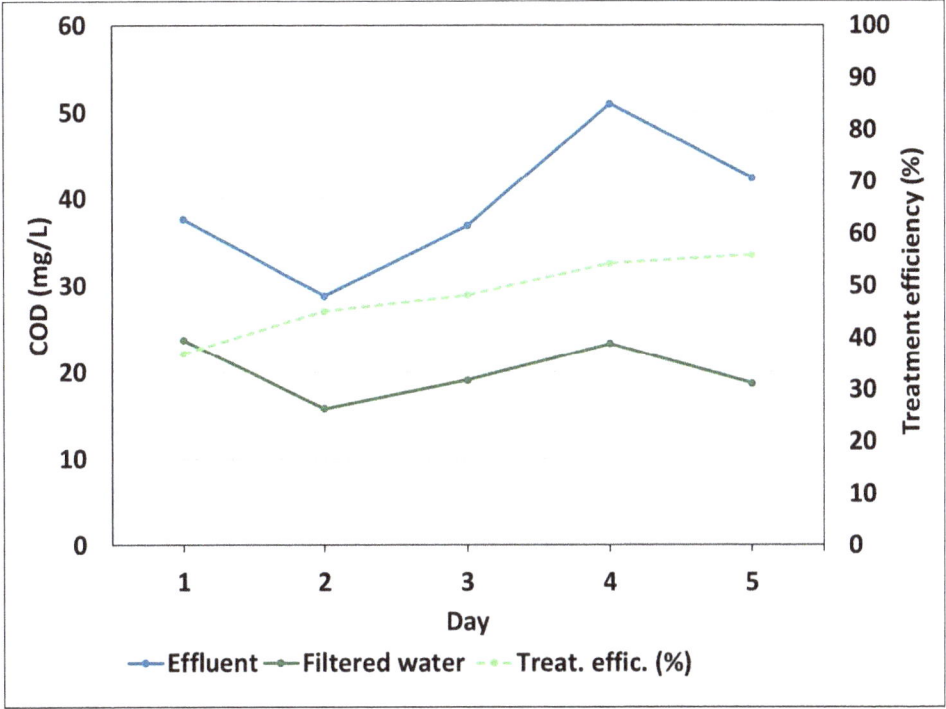

Figure 34: COD of effluent and treatment efficiency after microfiltration

7.3 BOD$_5$ removal from effluent using the MFO system

Determination of biochemical oxygen demand (BOD) is one of the oxidation methods for determining the amount of organic matter in water in which the oxidizing substance in water is dissolved oxygen. The mass concentration of dissolved oxygen is used (under t days at 20 °C) under certain conditions (with or without nitrification inhibition) for the biological oxidation of organic or inorganic substances (Roš & Zupančič, 2010). The average annual value of BOD$_5$ at the Shalek Valley fluent is 225 mg/L. Figure (Figure 35) shows the BOD$_5$ values in the inflow, which ranged from 49 mg/L to 186 mg/L. The average annual value of BOD$_5$ at the WWTP in the outflow is 25 mg/L. Prior to effluent microfiltration, values ranged from 10.4 mg/L to 20.2 mg/L. After microfiltration, the values decreased from 5.6 mg/L to 8.2 mg/L, which means that a cleansing effect of up to 59% was achieved, i.e., partial removal of BOD$_5$. The European Urban Wastewater Treatment Directive sets limit values for the concentration of BOD_5 in the effluent at 110 mg/L. The values of BOD_5 in the effluent after microfiltration are also in line with the new EU Regulation 2020/741 with minimum requirements for water reuse set at $\leq$10 mg/L.

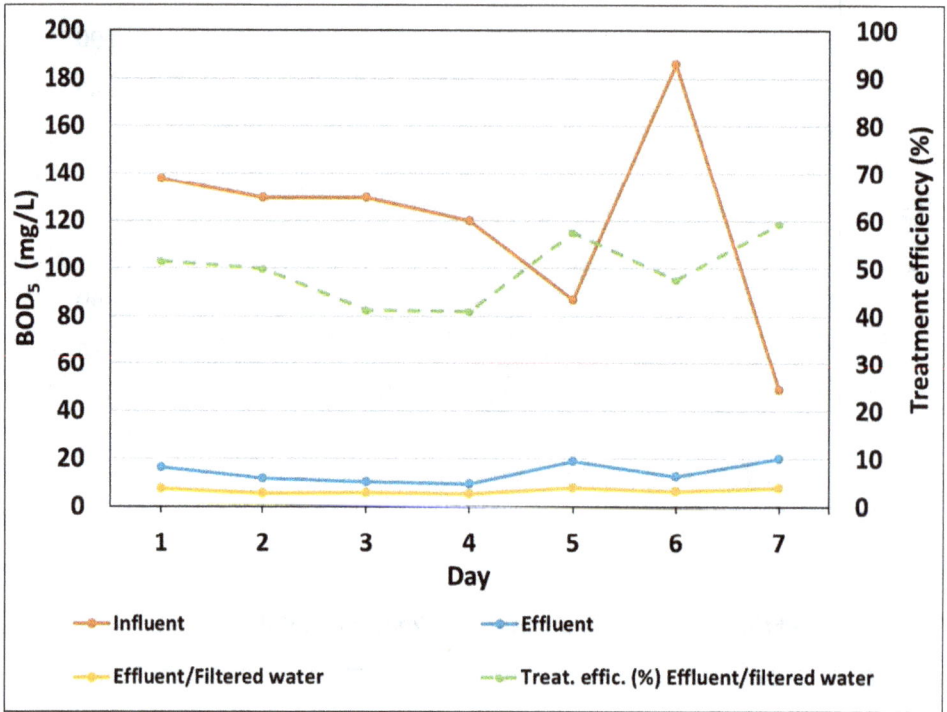

Figure 35: BOD5 values in the influent and effluent with the treatment efficiency after microfiltration

7.4 TSS values (mg/L) in the influent and effluent with the treatment efficiency after microfiltration

Wastewater contains a range of solid suspended solids (TSS) that vary in particle size, shape, and colloidal particles. Usually, 2/3 of all substances present in wastewater are in suspended form, the rest being dissolved matter (Roš & Zupančič, 2010). The TSS particle size is 10-4 mm or more. The average annual value of TSS at the inlet of the Shalek Valley WWTP is 161 mg/L. Before microfiltration, the inflow TSS ranged from 37 mg/L to 52 mg/L (Figure 36). After microfiltration, the TSS value decreased from 0.9 mg/L to 3 mg/L, which means that a cleansing effect of up to 97% was achieved. Thorough removal of TSS was achieved by microfiltration, but this type of inlet treatment does not make sense, as it does not remove biodegradable substances

(COD, BOD$_5$, NH$_4$-N, N-total, P-total), which are removed only by biological treatment.

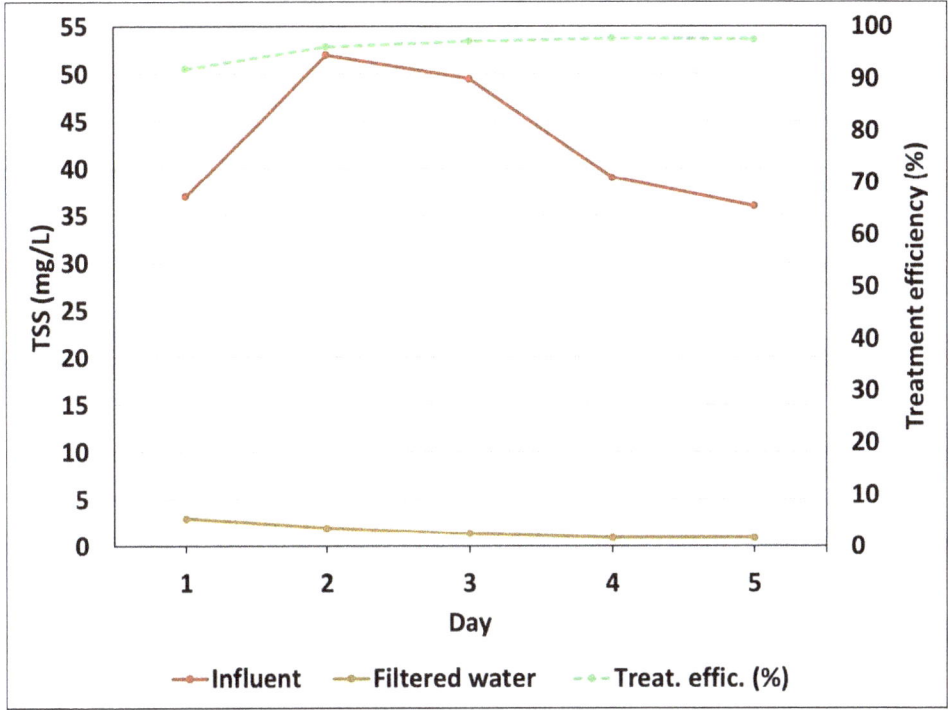

Figure 36: TSS values in the influent with a treatment efficiency after microfiltration

7.4.1 Analysis of microplastic particles and fibres in the influent - microscopic image

We tested the structure of the TSS according to the presence of microplastic particles and fibres. The analysis was performed with the MFO system to prepare 4 L of concentrate, i.e., 20% of the total wastewater (20 L). A portion of the concentrate (2 L) was passed through a felt filter microscopically imaged at 1600 x magnification. The microscopic image of the inlet (Figure 37) shows that the water was heavily loaded with suspended solids and plastic microfibres (residues on the felt).

Figure 37: Microscopic image of the influent (1600 x magnification)

7.4.2 Determination of the microplastics presence in the influent by FT-IR spectroscopy

A more detailed analysis to identify the microplastic particles was performed with an FT-IR spectrophotometer. The graph (Figure 38) shows that the absorption measurement showed two smaller signals at the wavenumbers 2920 cm^{-1} and 2845 cm^{-1} and a pronounced signal at the wave number 1030 cm^{-1} based on the literature means that ethylene-vinyl acetate (EVA) and polypropylene (PP) were present under these conditions as they represent the CH longitudinal valence wave characteristic of organic matter. The following smaller signals were shown at the wavenumbers 1634 cm^{-1} and 1538 cm^{-1} , representing the C = O bond characteristic of polyamides (PA), e.g., nylon. A smaller signal was shown at a wavenumber of 1452 cm^{-1}, which is characteristic of polystyrene (PS) and represents a CH$_2$ bond. Current practice shows that polypropylene (PP), ethylene-vinyl acetate (EVA), polystyrene (PS), polyethylene (PE), and polyamide (PA) are most commonly present in municipal wastewater

78

because of the use of cosmetics and machine washing of synthetic fabrics. Determination of the presence of microplastics in the influent by FT-IR spectroscopy.

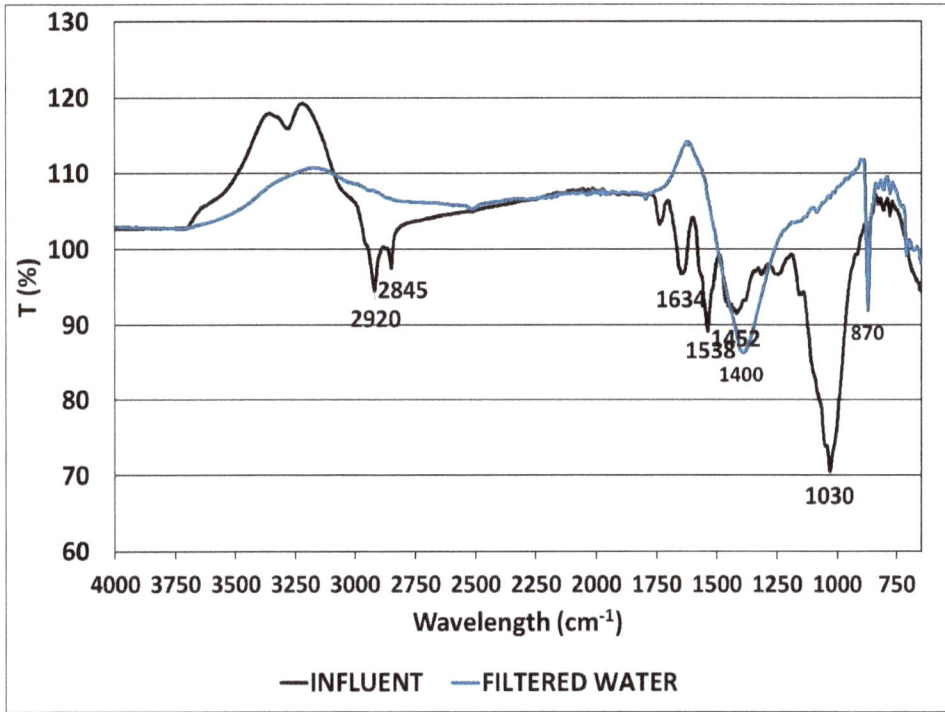

Figure 38: IR spectra of particles in the influent before and after microfiltration

After microfiltration, only two smaller signals appeared at the wavenumbers 1400 cm^{-1} and 870 cm^{-1}, which means that the membrane retained most of the particles described in this chapter (Figure 38). Based on the literature, these signals could not be assigned a suitable material, so they are considered as inorganic impurities or impurities of other polymeric materials. Smaller signals, however, are present due to noise.

7.5 TSS removal from the effluent using MFO system

The average annual value of TSS in the Shalek Valley WWTP of the effluent is 7.75 mg/L. Figure (Figure 39) shows the TSS values in the effluent before MFO treatment, 5.6 mg/L to 11.2 mg/L. After treating the effluent with MFO, the TSS values decreased from 0.9 mg/L to 1.4 mg/L, so a purification effect of up to 91% was achieved.

The European Urban Wastewater Treatment Directive sets limit values for TSS effluent concentrations at 35 mg/L. The results confirm the successful microfiltration, as the achieved TSS values are much lower than prescribed. TSS effluent values after microfiltration are also in line with the new EU Regulation 2020/741 on minimum requirements for water reuse, set at ≤10 mg/L.

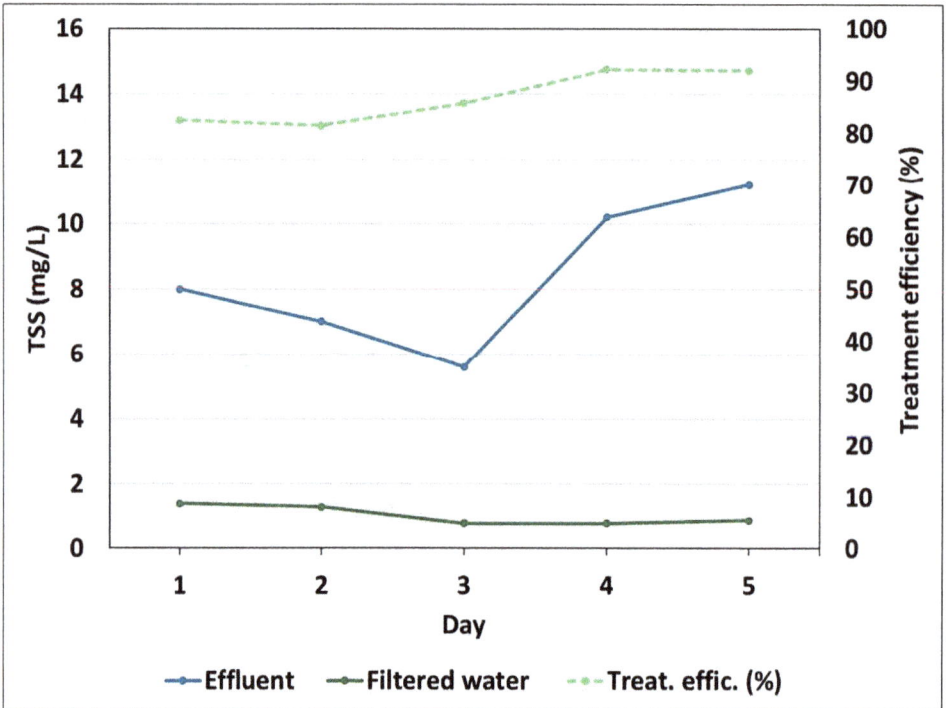

Figure 39: TSS in the effluent and treatment efficiency after microfiltration

7.5.1 Analysis of microplastic particles and fibres in the effluent - microscopic image

From the microscopic image at the outlet (Figure 40, Figure 41), the water was still heavily loaded with suspended solids and plastic microfibres (residues on the felt) after all stages of purification. Therefore, this water represents a point source of microplastic transfer to the natural aquatic environment. The figure (Figure 40) shows that after microfiltration of the effluent (filtered water), there are no TSS and microplastic residues on the felt, which means that the membrane retained virtually all TSS, including particles and microplastic fibres.

Figure 40: Microscopic image of the effluent (1600 × magnification)

Figure 41: Microscopic image of the filtered water (1600 × magnification)

7.5.2 Determination of the microplastics presence in the effluent by FT-IR spectroscopy

Chemical identification of microplastic particles was performed with an FT-IR spectrophotometer. From the graphical representation (Figure 42), smaller signals at the wave number 3298 cm^{-1} were shown when measuring the absorption, which, based on the literature (Jung et al., 2018, Medved, 2019), means that a hydrocarbon - polyamide (PA) was present under these conditions. The next, more significant signal was shown at the wave number 1377 cm^{-1}, which is characteristic of polypropylene (PP). The signal shown at the wavenumber 872 cm^{-1} could not be assigned a suitable material based on the literature, so it is a mixture of different polymeric materials, or the signal is due to noise.

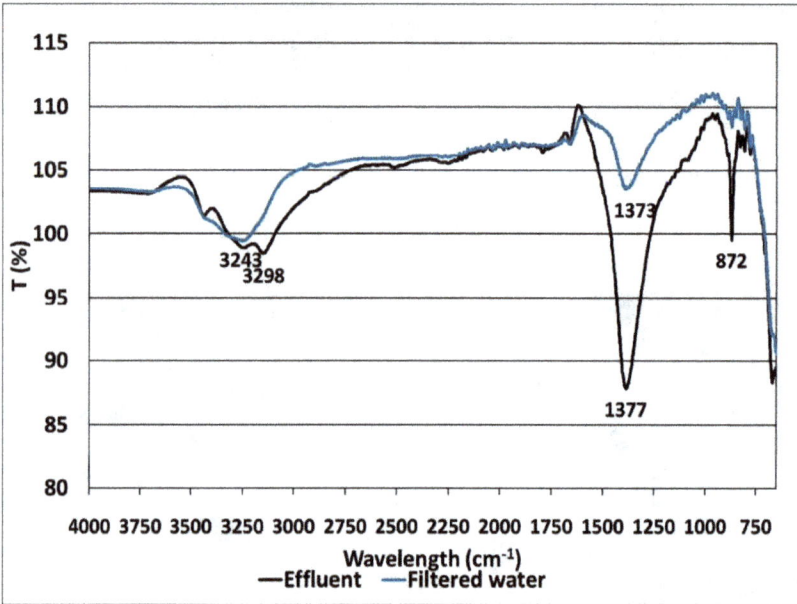

Figure 42: IR spectra of particles in the effluent before and after microfiltration

After microfiltration of the effluent, only two smaller signals appeared at the wavenumbers 3243 cm^{-1} and 1373 cm^{-1}, which means that the membrane retained most of the particles described in this section (Figure 42). However, given the low intensity in the spectrum, it is impossible to assign a suitable material to these signals based on the literature, as these are likely impurities of other materials, or the signal is due to noise.

7.6 Total nitrogen removal from the effluent using MFO system

Nitrogen compounds are present in the effluent in the form of organically bound nitrogen (N) and the form of ammonium nitrogen (NH₄–N). During biological wastewater treatment, the conversion of N to NH_4–N occurs with the help of microorganisms, which in the next phase, together with NH_4–N, is converted from nitrite (NO_2-N) to nitrate (NO_3-N). This process is called nitrification. Finally, part of the nitrogen compounds is converted into elemental nitrogen under anoxic conditions, i.e., without released oxygen (O_2), and is released into the air in the form of N_2. This process is called denitrification.

The average annual value of total nitrogen (N) in the Shalek Valley WWTP at the outflow is 10.6 mg/L. Prior to microfiltration, the value of N-total in the effluent ranged from 9.14 mg/L to 21 mg/L (Figure 43). After microfiltration, the value of N-total was reduced to 6 mg/L to 16.4 mg/L, which means that a cleansing effect of up to 34% was achieved. Only partial removal of total N was achieved by microfiltration, as nitrogen compounds in wastewater are present in dissolved form and are predominantly removed by biological treatment. The European Urban Wastewater Treatment Directive sets limit values for the concentration of N-total effluent at 15 mg/L. The results confirm the successful microfiltration, as the achieved N-total values are much lower than prescribed.

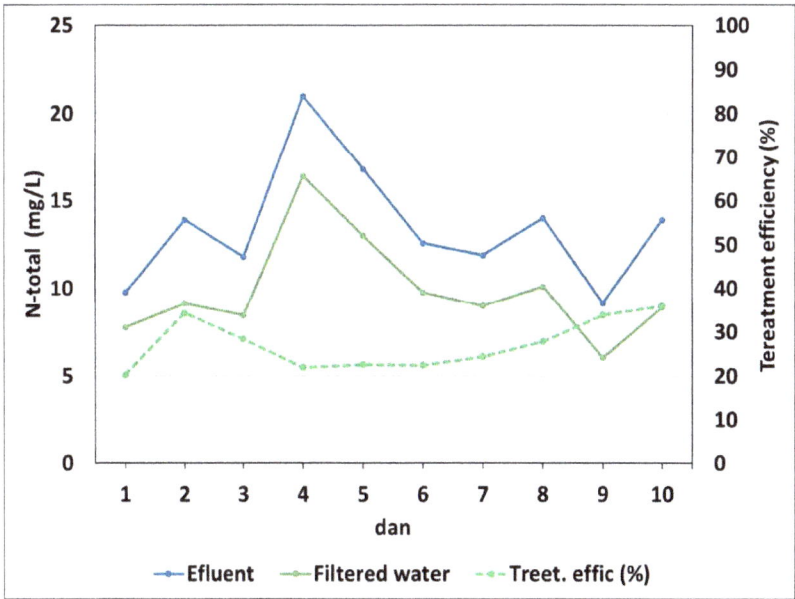

Figure 43: Total N values in effluent and treatment efficiency

7.7 Ammonium N (NH₄–N) treatment in the influent using MFO system

The average annual value of NH₄–N at the WWTP of the Shalek Valley in the discharge is 17.7 mg/L. Prior to microfiltration, the inflow NH₄–N value ranged from 14.4 mg/L to 27.7 mg/L (Figure 44). After microfiltration, the NH₄–N value decreased from 8.7 mg/L to 11.5 mg/L, which means that a cleansing effect of up to 58% was achieved. Only partial removal of NH₄–N was achieved by microfiltration, as nitrogen compounds are present in the wastewater in dissolved form and are largely removed by biological treatment.

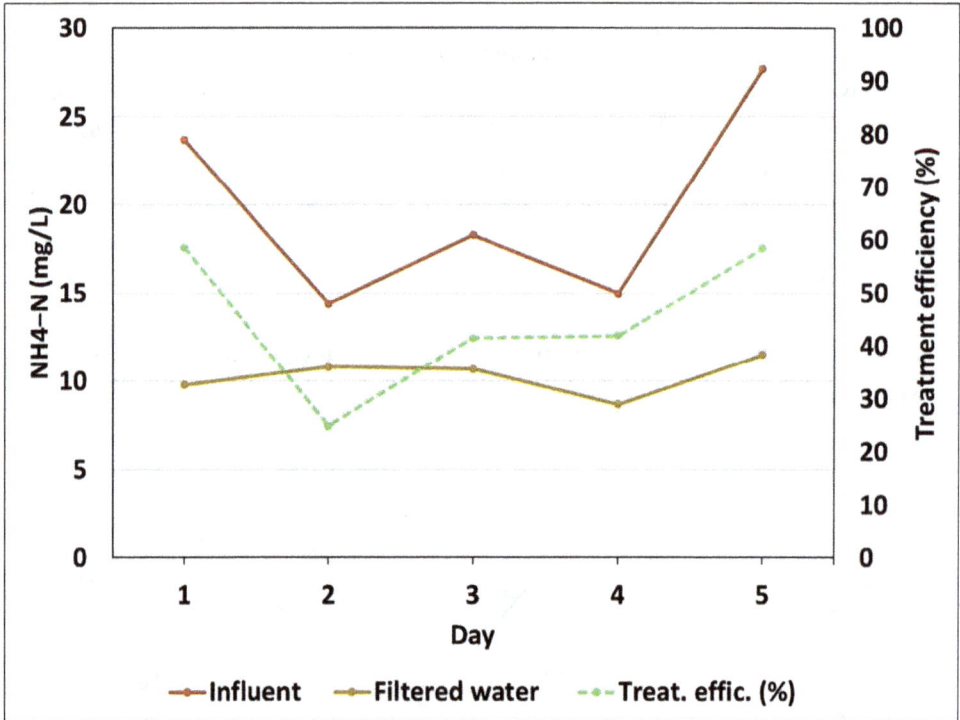

Figure 44: NH₄–N values in the influent and treatment efficiency after microfiltration

7.8 Ammonium nitrogen (NH₄–N) treatment from effluent using MFO system

The average annual value of NH_4–N at the Shalek Valley WWTP in the outflow is 1.12 mg/L. Figure (Figure 45) shows the NH_4–N values in the effluent before microfiltration ranged from 0.6 mg/L to 2.25 mg/L. After microfiltration, the NH_4–N values decreased from 0.35 mg/L to 1.72 mg/L, so a cleansing effect of up to 41.6% was achieved. Only partial removal of total NH_4–N was achieved by microfiltration, as nitrogen compounds are present in the wastewater in dissolved form and are mostly removed by biological treatment.

The European Urban Wastewater Treatment Directive sets limit values for NH_4–N effluent concentrations at 10 mg/L. The results confirm successful microfiltration, as the achieved NH_4–N values are much lower than prescribed.

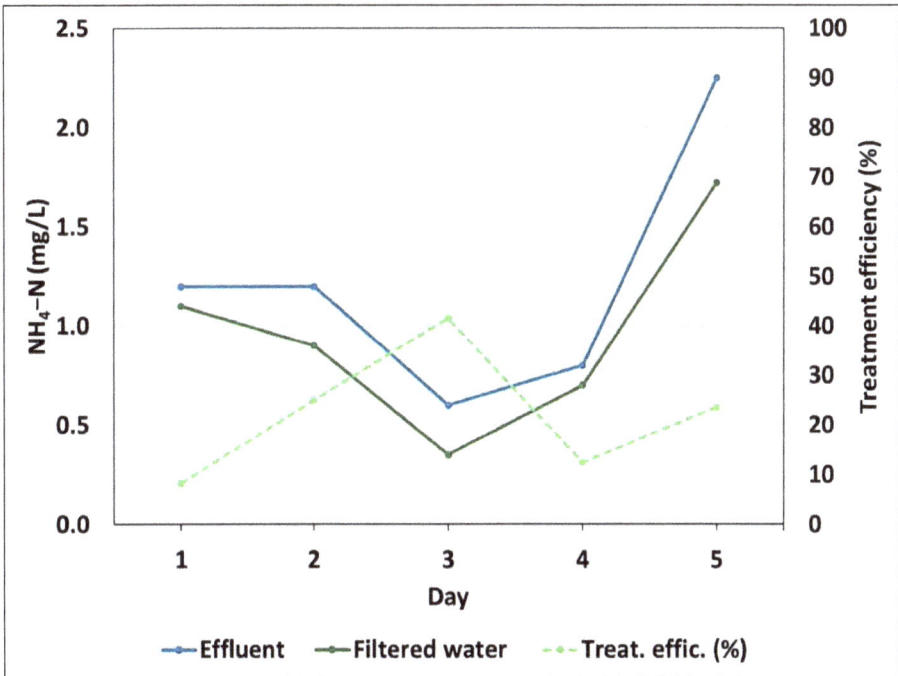

Figure 45: NH₄–N values in the effluent and treatment efficiency after microfiltration

7.9 Total P removal from the effluent using MFO system

The average annual value of P-total at the Shalek Valley WWTP in the outflow is 1.26 mg/L. The figure (Figure 46) shows the P-total values in the effluent before microfiltration, which ranged from 0.71 mg/L to 1.74 mg/L. After effluent microfiltration, the P-total values decreased from 0.59 mg/L to 1.26 mg/L, so a cleansing effect of up to 42% was achieved. However, only partial removal of total P was achieved by microfiltration, as the phosphorus compounds in the wastewater are present in dissolved form and are predominantly removed by biological treatment.

The European Urban Wastewater Treatment Directive sets limit values for the concentration of P-total effluent at 2 mg/L. The results confirm the successful microfiltration, as the achieved values of P-total are much lower than prescribed.

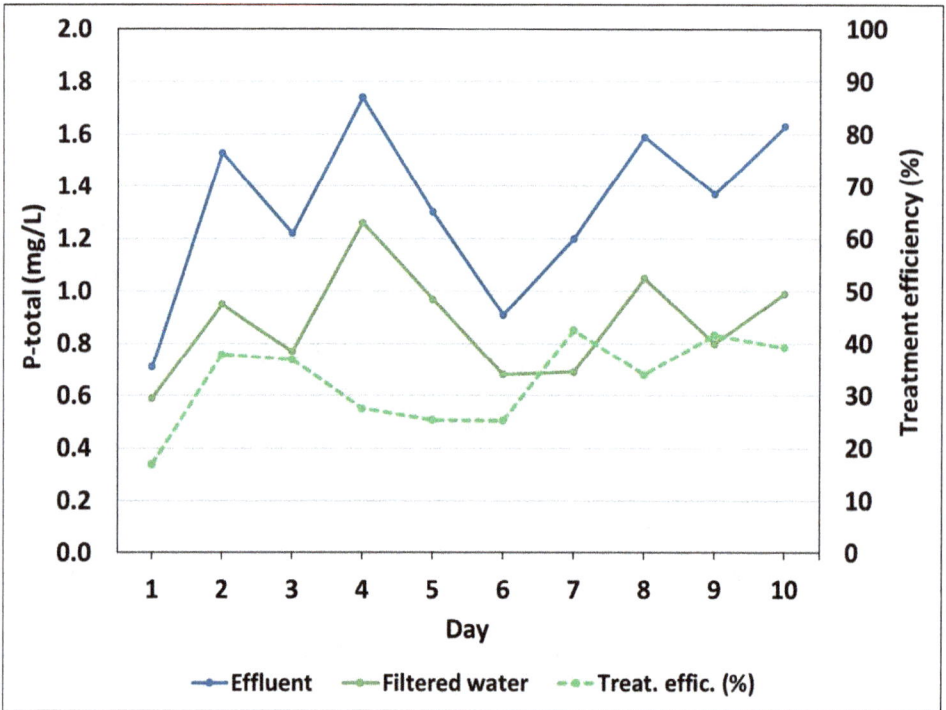

Figure 46: Total P values in the effluent and treatment efficiency after microfiltration

7.10 Additional effluent treatment using MFO system

In addition to microfiltration, the MFO system also enables additional treatment with ozone (O_3). The system is simple, as it does not require high pressures for filtration, and in parallel, allows good ozonation (disinfection).

7.10.1 COD values in the effluent after microfiltration and ozonation using MFO system

The results show (Figure 47) that the COD value in the effluent before MFO treatment ranged from 38 mg/L to 45.1 mg/L. After microfiltration, the value decreased from 12.4 mg/L to 13.8 mg/L, which means that a cleansing effect of up to 68.74% was achieved. After ozonation, the COD value ranged from 11.6 mg/L to 12.4 mg/L, and a cleansing effect of up to 74.28 was achieved, i.e., an additional 5.5% COD was removed by ozonation.

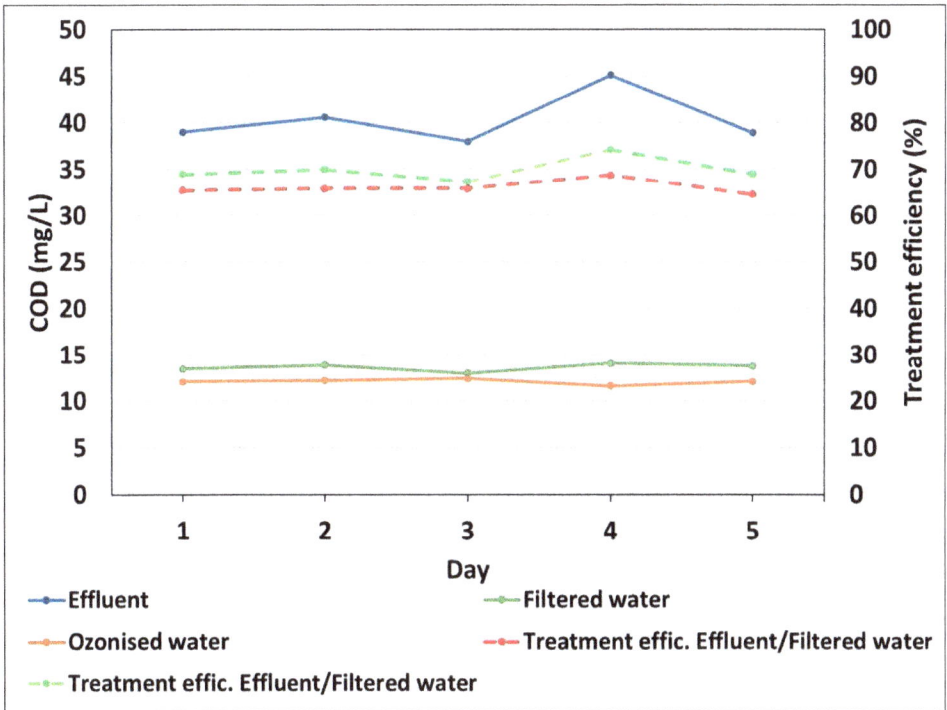

Figure 47: COD values of the effluent and treatment efficiency using MFO system

7.10.2 TSS values in the effluent after microfiltration and ozonation using MFO system

It can be seen from the figure (Figure 48) that the TSS value in the effluent before MFO treatment ranged from 6.6 mg/L to 14 mg/L. After microfiltration, the value decreased from 0.3 mg/L to 0.5 mg/L, which means that a cleaning effect of up to 97.56% was achieved. After ozonation, the TSS value and the cleaning effect did not change, which means that the ozonation was zero, as the membrane already retained practically all particles.

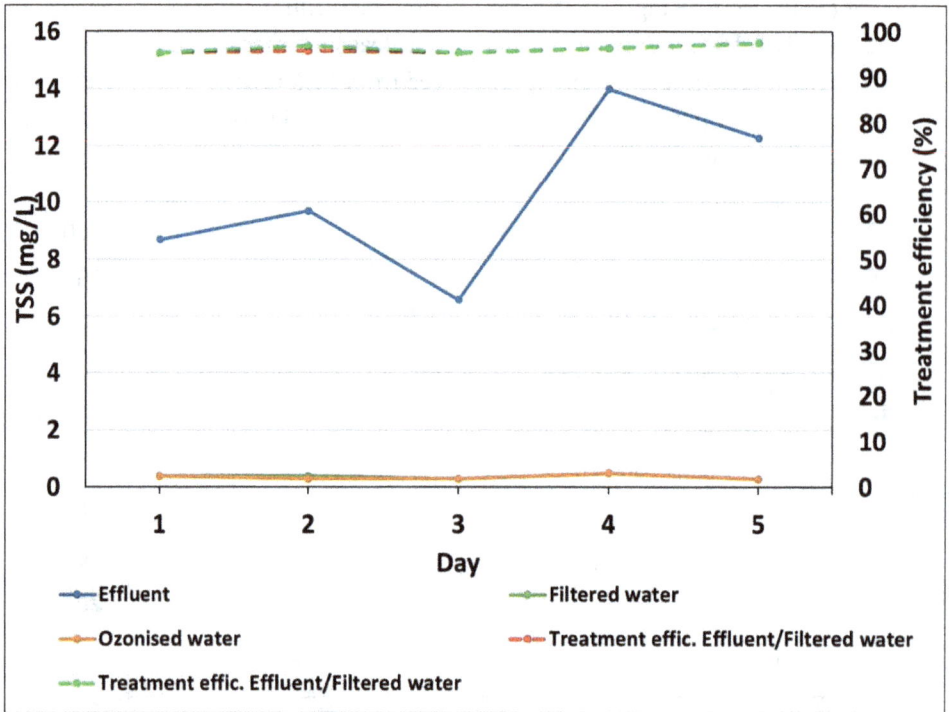

Figure 48: TSS values of the effluent and treatment efficiency using MFO system

7.10.3 Total N values in the effluent after microfiltration and ozonation using MFO system

Prior to MFO treatment, N-total values ranged from 13.9 mg/L to 15.8 mg/L. After microfiltration, the values decreased from 5.9 mg/L to 9.8 mg/L, meaning that 57.24% of the N-total was removed. After ozonation, the N-total value decreased from 5.9 mg/L to 9.46 mg/L, which means that approx. 3% N-total removal (Figure 49).

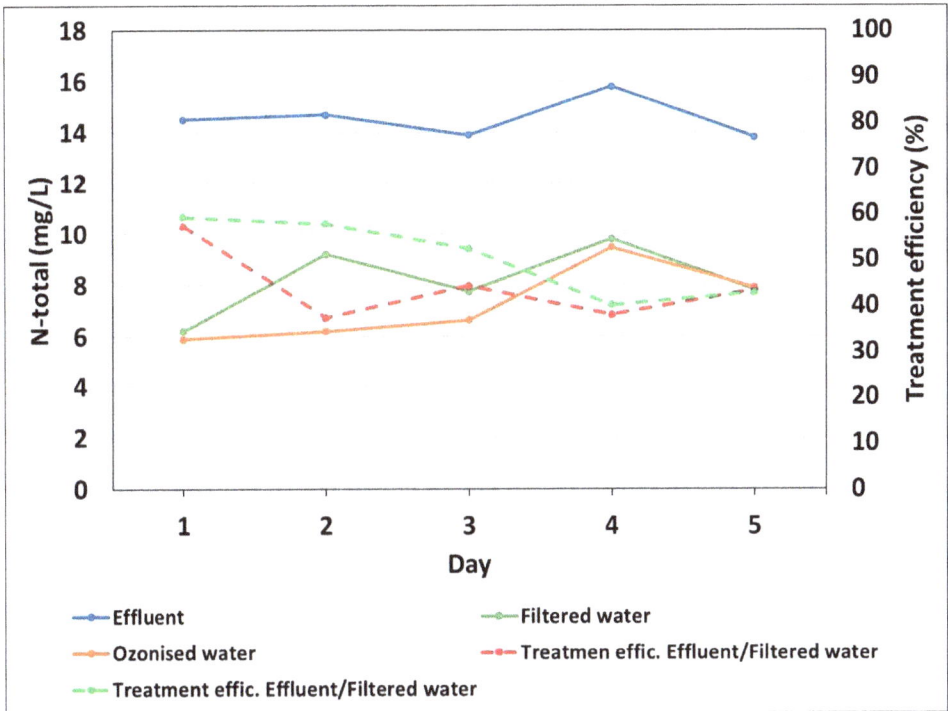

Figure 49: N-total values in the effluent and treatment efficiency using MFO system

7.10.4P-total values in the effluent after microfiltration and ozonation using MFO system

Prior to MFO treatment, P-total values ranged from 1.22 mg/L to 1.43 mg/L. After microfiltration, the values decreased from 0.44 mg/L to 0.49 mg/L, meaning that 67.13% of the P-total was removed. After ozonation, the N-total value ranged from 0.36 mg/L to 0.61 mg/L, indicating that ozonation had no effect on the P-total (Figure 50).

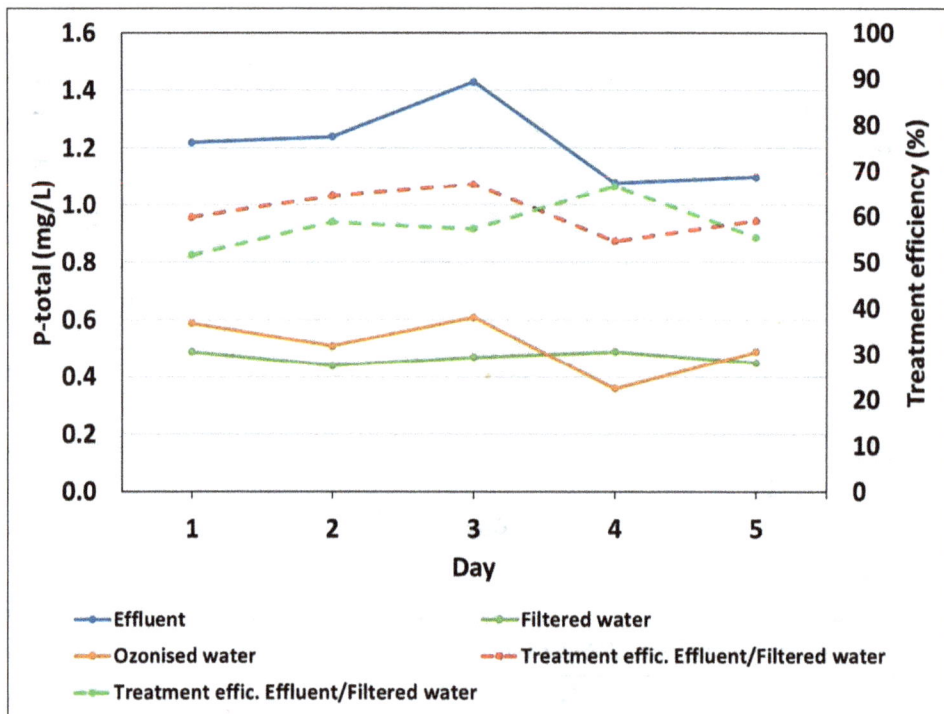

Figure 50: P-total values in the effluent and treatment efficiency using MFO system

7.10.5 Values of total coliform bacteria in the effluent after microfiltration and ozonation using the MFO system

The value of total coliform bacteria at the effluent was > 200.5 MPN/100 mL. After microfiltration, e value was reduced from 23.1 MPN/100 mL to 40.6 MPN/100 mL, indicating a purification effect of 79.7% to 88%. Therefore, according to EU Regulation 2020/741, this water would be classified in B quality class of processed water. After disinfection with ozone, the value of coliform bacteria decreased to <1 MPN/100 mL. It means that the cleaning effect was 100%. Therefore, according to the regulation (EU Regulation 2020/741), this water would be ranked in the best A quality class of processed water (Figure 51). It means that the treated wastewater thus meets all the criteria for irrigation in agriculture, which are legally defined by categories A to D. The legislation allows water to be used for other purposes, e.g., in industry, for recreational purposes, and in the field of the environment.

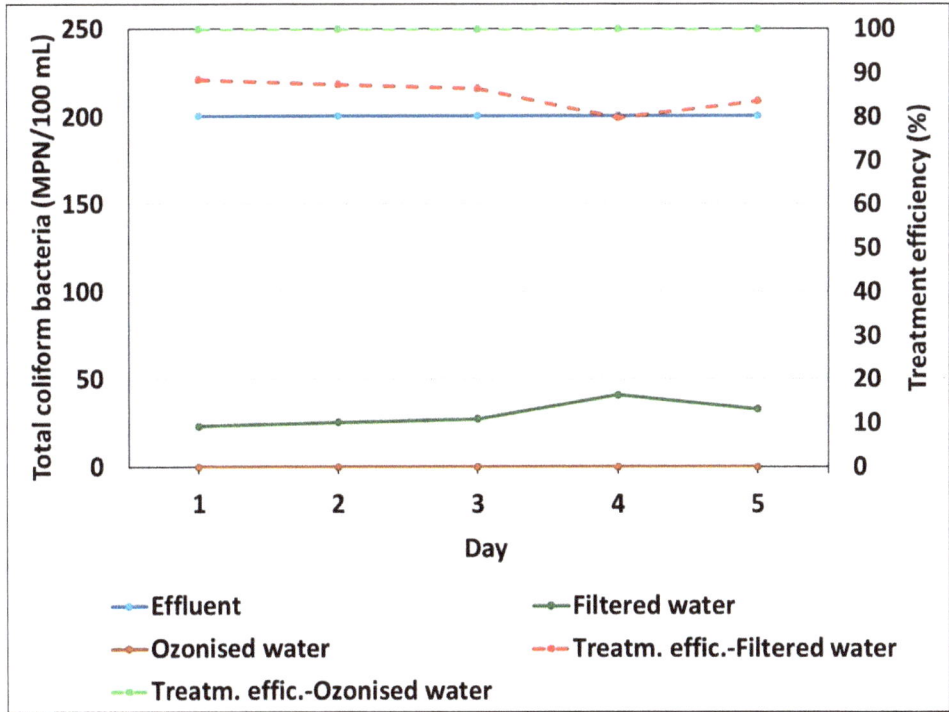

Figure 51: Values of total coliform bacteria in the effluent and treatment efficiency using MFO system

7.10.6 Values of E. coli in the effluent after microfiltration and ozonation using the MFO system

The value of *Escherichia coli* at effluent was > 200.5 MPN/100 mL. After microfiltration, the value decreased from 13.2 MPN/100 mL to 14.8 MPN/100 mL, meaning that the cleaning effect was up to 93%. According to EU Regulation 2020/741, this water would be classified in B quality class of processed water. After disinfection with ozone, the value of *E. coli* decreased to <1 MPN/100 mL, which means that the cleaning effect was 100% and according to the regulation this water would be ranked in the best A quality class of processed water (Figure 52). This means that the treated wastewater thus meets all the criteria for irrigation in agriculture, which are legally defined by categories A to D. The legislation allows water to be used for other purposes as well, e.g., in industry, for recreational purposes, and in the field of the environment.

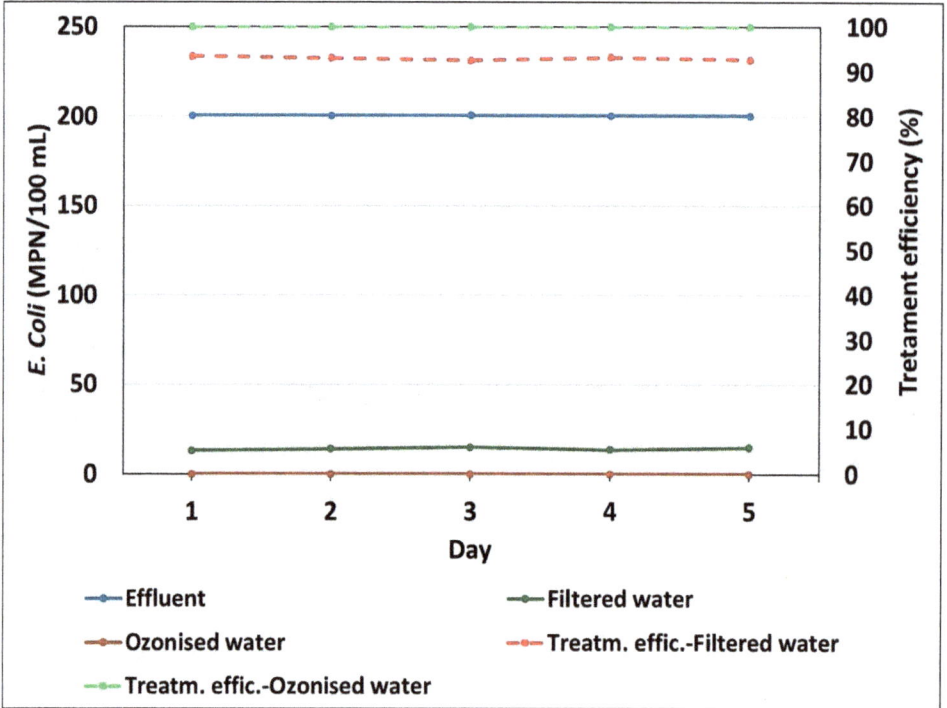

Figure 52: Values of E. coli of effluent and treatment efficiency using MFO system

These tests confirm that a microfiltration system with an ozone generator (MFO) can treat wastewater very efficiently. Suspended matter (TSS), including microplastics, was removed by membrane filtration up to 97%, COD was removed by up to 55%, nitrogen (N), and phosphorus (P) were removed by 57% to 67%. Bacteriological analysis showed that the cleansing effect after membrane filtration was up to 88% relative to total coliform bacteria and 93% relative to *E. coli*. After additional ozonation of the filtered water, a 100% cleansing effect was achieved for coliform bacteria and *E. coli*. From a chemical and bacteriological point of view, such treated water meets the minimum requirements for the reuse of treated water from municipal wastewater treatment plants set by European legislation (EU Regulation 2020/741). The MFO system could be introduced in treatment plants, as it would reduce the point source of TSS and microplastics transfer to watercourses, and water could be reused for irrigation in agriculture (in all categories) and in industry, for recreational purposes and environment.

8   Industrial wastewater treatment using SiC membrane filtration

We installed a treatment plant for the dairy industry, in which we installed a SiC membrane filter instead of a secondary settler. The treatment plant proved to be extremely successful, as we removed most of the organic matter and TSS. Let's look at the effect of the treatment plant.

The characteristics of industrial wastewater was as follows:

pH = 8,4

COD = 2300 mg/L

BOD_5 = 1570 mg/L

Total suspended solids = 320 mg/L

N-total = 76 mg/L

P-total = 17,7 mg/L

Q = 54 m^3/L

We introduced equalisation tank and sequencing batch reactor (SBR) with membrane SiC filter.

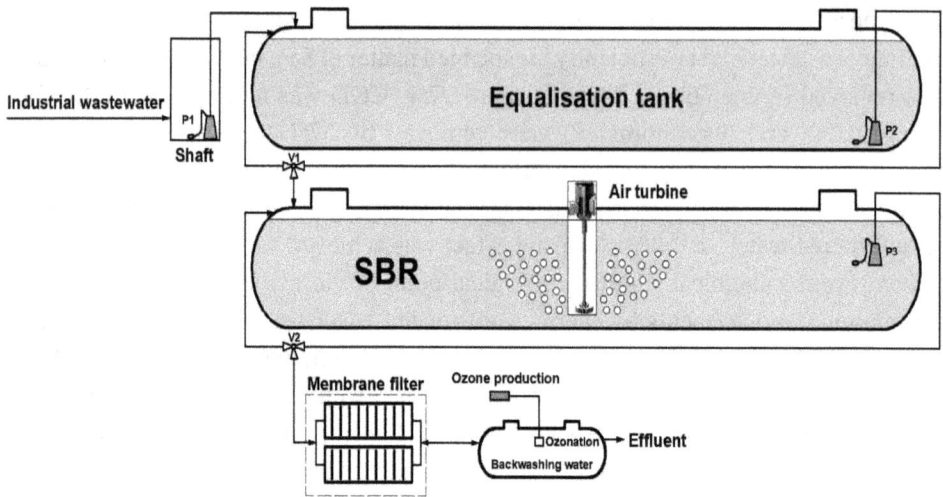

Figure 53: System for industrial wastewater treatment

Equalisation tank

The wastewater equalisation tank (volume 50 m^3), is equipped with a submersible pump (P2), which has a dual purpose:

- mixes and thus homogenizes wastewater. It pumps water from the back to the front of the tank.
- Occasionally pumps wastewater into the SBR via a three-way valve (V1) when the reactor is ready to receive wastewater.

The submersible pump (P2) has a level switch to operate if there is enough water in the tank.

Wastewater treatment in SBR

The biological stage has a volume of 50 m^3 and serves as a batch reactor (SBR). A submersible pump (Č3) is installed in the reactor, which is slightly raised.

The operation of the SBR works as follows. First, a certain amount of wastewater (P2) is pumped into the reactor, mixed, and allowed to decompose some organic matter. Then, after a specific time, turn on the ventilation (P3), which serves for good homogenization of the contents (mixing) and further decomposition of organic matter present in the wastewater. After a specific time, stop aerating and mixing the contents to settle the stool actively. After a particular time, turn on the pump (P3) via the three-way valve (V2), and direct the contents into the membrane filter. The treated water drains into the drain channel, which leads to the municipal treatment plant. Once the water content, which must be the same as we added in the first stage, is removed, the cycle can be repeated.

SBR working phases

For regular SBR operation, we suggest the following operating mode:

1. The SBR must contain activated sludge with a concentration of 6-8 g/L. The activated sludge suspension can be initiated from a municipal sewage treatment plant.
2. 20 m³ of wastewater is pumped into the reactor (SBR) by a submersible pump installed in the containment reactor (P2). The pump flow is about 40 m³/h. In parallel, the submersible pump in SBR (P3) is running for 1.5 hours.
3. After 1.5 hours, the Toring turbine is switched on and aerate the activated sludge suspension. This phase lasts 3.5 hours.
4. After this phase (3.5 hours of ventilation), the turbine and the submersible pump (P3) is switched off to allow the activated sludge to settle. This phase lasts 0.5 hours.
5. When the activated sludge settles, the submersible pump (P3) is switched on, and the flow is diverted via the three-way valve (V2) to the diaphragm filter. This phase lasts until 20 m³ of water is pumped, presumably half an hour.
6. If there is sufficient wastewater during the retention period, points 2 to 5 shall be repeated.
7. If there is insufficient wastewater in the containment reactor, the system (SBR) is idle.

The entire phase of SBR operation lasts 6.0 hours, so that we can do 4 phases in one day. So, we could treat a maximum of 80 m³ of wastewater per day.

Treatment efficiency

The characteristics of the effluent were as follows:

pH = 8,4

COD = 80 mg/L

BOD_5 = < 10 mg/L

Total suspended solids = < 0.5 mg/L

N-total = < 10 mg/L

P-total = < 1.0 mg/L

Treatment efficiency is as follows:

> 96.5 % according to COD,

> 99,3 % according to BOD_5,

> 99,8 % according to TSS,

> 86.8 % according to total N,

> 94.7 % according to total P.

The main advantage of such treatment is that there is no need to build a sizeable secondary settler. But, at the same time, most organic matter and, above all, practically all TSS is removed.

9 Conclusions

In recent years, wastewater treatment has increasingly focused on combination with membrane treatment and biological treatment and disinfection or oxidation of the remaining components in the treated water. Due to the relatively complicated use of synthetic membranes (clogging, wear, sensitivity to corrosive chemicals), ceramic membranes are becoming more and more popular.

The application of ceramic membrane technology in water and wastewater treatment is rapidly growing. Inherent advantages of the ceramic membrane, including chemical and thermal stability, low fouling propensity and long lifespan, make ceramic membrane technology attractive. Furthermore, the Ceramic membranes could be integrated with advanced oxidation processes such as in-situ ozonation that cannot be applied in the case of the polymeric membrane due to their potential degradation during long-term exposure. In addition, the hybrid-ceramic membrane processes such as ceramic membrane bioreactor are superior to polymeric counterparts due to higher flux, higher pollutant removal, lower fouling rate and higher cleaning efficiency. Although ceramic membrane has a high capital cost, life-cycle costs of ceramic and polymeric plants are comparable.

We have shown the theoretical foundations of filtration, emphasizing ceramic membranes in combination with wastewater treatment and drinking water preparation.

10 Literature

Aani, S. F. Mustafa, T. N. Hilal, N. (2020). Ultrafiltration membranes for wastewater and water process engineering: A comprehensive statistical review over the past decade, Journal of Water Process Engineering. 35, 101241.

Al Aani, S., Mustafa, T. N., & Hilal, N. (2020). Ultrafiltration membranes for wastewater and water process engineering: A comprehensive statistical review over the past decade. *Journal of Water Process Engineering, 35*. doi:10.1016/j.jwpe.2020.101241

Anis, S. F., Hashaikeh, R., & Hilal, N. (2019). Microfiltration membrane processes: A review of research trends over the past decade. *Journal of Water Process Engineering, 32*. doi:10.1016/j.jwpe.2019.100941

Asif, M. B., & Zhang, Z. (2021). Ceramic membrane technology for water and wastewater treatment: A critical review of performance, full-scale applications, membrane fouling and prospects. *Chemical Engineering Journal, 418*. doi:10.1016/j.cej.2021.129481

Banjamin, M. M., & Lawler, D. F. (2013). *Water Quality Engineering; Physical / Chemical Treatment Processes*. Hoboken: Willey.

Bayo, J., Olmos, S., & López-Castellanos, J. (2021). Assessment of Microplastics in a Municipal Wastewater Treatment Plant With Tertiary Treatment: Removal E. *Research square*, 1-22. doi:10.21203/rs.3.rs-258840/v1

Brief, T. (2021). Filtration. Available from https://water-research.net/Waterlibrary/privatewell/filtration.pdf (Accesed 5. October 2021).

C. Lubello, C., Gor, R., de Bernardinis, A. M., & Simonelli, G. (2003). Ultrafiltration as tertiary treatment for industrial reuse. *Water Science and Technology, 3*(4), 161-168.

Campanale, C., Massarelli, C., Savino, I., Locaputo, V., & Uricchio, V. F. (2020). A Detailed Review Study on Potential Effects of Microplastics and Additives of Concern on Human Health. *Int J Environ Res Public Health, 17*(4). doi:10.3390/ijerph17041212

Cembrane. (2021a). Cembrane technology. Available from https://www.cembrane.com/technology-1 (Accessed 7. July 2021).

Cembrane. (2021b). Cembrane-Operation and maintenance. Available from http://www.inwaters.com/resource/www/pdf/0301.pdf (Accessed 7. July 2021).

Cembrane. (2021c). New generation membranes. Available from https://stateo fgreen.com/en/partners/cembrane-new-generation-ceramic-membrane/ (Accessed 7. July 2021).

Chen, M., Shang, R., Sberna, P. M., Luiten-Olieman, M. W. J., Rietveld, L. C., & Heijman, S. G. J. (2020). Highly permeable silicon carbide-alumina ultrafiltration membranes for oil-in-water filtration produced with low-pressure chemical vapor deposition. *Separation and Purification Technology, 253.* doi:10.1016/j.seppur.2020.117496

Cowger, W., Gray, A. B., Eriksen, M., Moore, C., & Thiel, M. (2019). Evaluating wastewater effluent as a source of microplastics in environmental samples. In *Microplastics in Water and Wastewater* (pp. 109-131).

Digka, N., Tsangaris, C., Kaberi, H., Adamopoulou, A., & Zeri, C. (2018). Microplastic Abundance and Polymer Types in a Mediterranean Environment. In *Proceedings of the International Conference on Microplastic Pollution in the Mediterranean Sea* (pp. 17-24).

Enfrin, M., Dumee, L. F., & Lee, J. (2019). Nano/microplastics in water and wastewater treatment processes - Origin, impact and potential solutions. *Water Res, 161*, 621-638. doi:10.1016/j.watres.2019.06.049

EU Directive 91/271/EEC. (1991). Council Directive concerning urban water treatment. Available from https://www.eea.europa.eu/policy-documents/coun cil-directive-91-271-eec (Accessed 1. september 2021).

EU Regulation 2020/741 of the European Parliament and of the Council on minimum requirements for water reuse, pp. 4-20, 2020.

Fileder. (2021). Depth-Filtration-Brochure. Retrieved from https://www.fileder.co.uk/ fileder-app/app-uploads/2020/05/Depth-Filtration-Brochure.pdf

Gabelman, A. (2017). Crossflow Membrane Filtration Essentials. *Chemical Engineering*, 49-59.

Gao, J. (2016). *Membrane Separation Technology for Wastewater Treatment and its Study Progress and Development Trend*. Paper presented at the 4th International Conference on Mechanical Materials and Manufacturing Engineering.

Gunt. (2021). Basic knowledge of filtration. Available from https://www.gunt.de /images/download/filtration_water_english.pdf (Accessed 3. July 2021).

Habib, R. Z., Thiemann, T., & Al Kendi, R. (2020). Microplastics and Wastewater Treatment Plants—A Review. *Journal of Water Resource and Protection, 12*(01), 1-35. doi:10.4236/jwarp.2020.121001

Hansen, S. F., Hogan, S. A., Tobin, J., Rasmussen, J. T., Larsen, L. B., & Wiking, L. (2020). Microfiltration of raw milk for production of high-purity milk fat globule membrane material. *Journal of Food Engineering, 276*. doi:10.1016/j.jfoodeng. 2019.109887

Herzke, D., Ghaffari, P., Sundet, J. H., Tranang, C. A., & Halsband, C. (2021). Microplastic Fiber Emissions From Wastewater Effluents: Abundance, Transport Behavior and Exposure Risk for Biota in an Arctic Fjord. *Frontiers in Environmental Science, 9*. doi:10.3389/fenvs.2021.662168

Hu, L. C., Yen, W. H., Su, J. H., Chiang, M. Y., Wen, Z. H., Chen, W. F., . . . Sung, P. J. (2013). Cembrane derivatives from the soft corals, Sinularia gaweli and Sinularia flexibilis. *Mar Drugs, 11*(6), 2154-2167. doi:10.3390/md11062154

Hube, S., Eskafi, M., Hrafnkelsdottir, K. F., Bjarnadottir, B., Bjarnadottir, M. A., Axelsdottir, S., & Wu, B. (2020). Direct membrane filtration for wastewater treatment and resource recovery: A review. *Sci Total Environ, 710*, 136375. doi:10.1016/j.scitotenv.2019.136375

Ishaq, M. S., Afcheen, Y., Khan, A.Photocatalzsts/Applications and Attributes: Disinfection Methods

Jung, M.R., Horgen, F.D., Orski, S.V., Rodriguez, V., Beers, K.L., Balazsc, G.H., Jones, T.T., Workd, T.M., Brignac, K.C., Royer, S.M., Hyrenbacha, K.D., Jensen, B.A.,Jennifer Lynch, J.M., "Validation of ATR FT-IR to identify polymers of plastic marine debris, including those ingested by marine organisms," Marine Pollution Bulletin, vol. 127, pp. 704-716, 2018/02/01/ 2018, doi: https://doi.org/10.1016/j.marpolbul.2017.12.061

Koelmans, A. A., Mohamed Nor, N. H., Hermsen, E., Kooi, M., Mintenig, S. M., & De France, J. (2019). Microplastics in freshwaters and drinking water: Critical review and assessment of data quality. *Water Res, 155*, 410-422. doi:10.1016/j.watres.2019.02.054

Lebreton, L., & Andrady, A. (2019). Future scenarios of global plastic waste generation and disposal. *Palgrave Communications, 5*(1). doi:10.1057/s41599-018-0212-7

Li, Y., Zhang, Y., Chen, G., Xu, K., Gong, H., Huang, K., . . . Wang, J. (2021). Microplastics in Surface Waters and Sediments from Guangdong Coastal Areas, South China. *Sustainability, 13*(5). doi:10.3 390/su13052691

Liu, W., Zhang, J., Liu, H., Guo, X., Zhang, X., Yao, X., . . . Zhang, T. (2021). A review of the removal of microplastics in global wastewater treatment plants: Characteristics and mechanisms. *Environ Int, 146*, 106277. doi:10.1016/j.envint.2020.106277

Mameda, N., Park, H., & Choo, K.-H. (2020). Hybrid electrochemical microfiltration treatment of reverse osmosis concentrate: A mechanistic study on the effects of electrode materials. *Desalination, 493*. doi:10.1016/j.desal.2020.114617

Manouchehri, M., & Kargari, A. (2017). Water recovery from laundry wastewater by the cross flow microfiltration process: A strategy for water recycling in residential buildings. *Journal of Cleaner Production, 168*, 227-238. doi:10.1016/j.jclepro.2017.08.211

Medved, T.,"Comparison of the content of microplastics in wastewater and waste sludge of municipal wastewater treatment plants (in Slovenian) " University of Maribor, Faculty of Mechanical Engineering, pp. 37-53, 2019.

Mendret, J., Azais, A., Favier, T., & Brosillon, S. (2019). Urban wastewater reuse using a coupling between nanofiltration and ozonation: Techno-economic assessment. *Chemical Engineering Research and Design, 145*, 19-28. doi:10.1016/j.cherd.2019.02.034

Mouratib, R., Achiou, B., Krati, M. E., Younssi, S. A., & Tahiri, S. (2020). Low-cost ceramic membrane made from alumina- and silica-rich water treatment sludge and its application to wastewater filtration. *Journal of the European Ceramic Society, 40*(15), 5942-5950. doi:10.1016/j.jeurceramsoc.2020.07.050

Nathan, J. S. J., Shivanandappa, K. C., Sundran, B., Venkataramana, K. N., & Mani, K. R. (2008). Filtration Technique in Vaccine Manufacturing. *Advanced Bioteh*, 37-41.

Nqombolo, A., Mpupa, A., Moutloali, R. M., & Nomngongo, P. N. (2018). Wastewater Treatment Using Membrane Technology. In *Wastewater and Water Quality*.

Obotey Ezugbe, E., & Rathilal, S. (2020). Membrane Technologies in Wastewater Treatment: A Review. *Membranes (Basel), 10*(5). doi:10.3390/membranes 100 50089

Rihter Pikl, J., Lobnik, A., Uranjek, N. & Roš, M. (2021). Application of membrane filtration-ozonation system for additional water treatment. Int J Eng Sci, 10, 48-56. doi:10.9790/1813-1003024856

Roš, M., & Zupančič, D. G. (2010). *Wastewater Treatment (in Slovenian)*. Velenje: College of Environmental Protection, Velenje.

Saipolbahri, N., Bitlus, M. L. A., Isamil, N. A., Fauzi, N. M., & Subky, N. S. (2020). *Determination of Microplastics in Surface Water and Sediment of Kelantan Bay*. Paper presented at the 2nd International Conference on Tropical Resources and Sustainable Sciences, City campus, Malaysia.

Saqib Ishaq, M., Afsheen, Z., Khan, A., & Khan, A. (2018). Disinfection Methods. In *Photocatalysts - Applications and Attributes*.

Sastri, V. S., Ghali, E., Elboujdanini, M. (2007). Corrosion Prevention and Protection: Practical Solution. Hoboken: Willey.

Schlosser, Š. (2014). Membrane Filtration. In *Engineering Aspects of Food Biotechnology* (pp. 145-182).

Talvitie, J., Mikola, A., Koistinen, A., & Setala, O. (2017). Solutions to microplastic pollution - Removal of microplastics from wastewater effluent with advanced wastewater treatment technologies. *Water Res, 123,* 401-407. doi:10.1016/j.watres.2017.07.005

Tchobanoglous, G., Burton, F. L., & Stensel, H. D. (2003). *Wastewater Engineering; Treatment and Reuse.* Boston: McGraw Hill.

Thomas, D., Schütze, B., Heinze, W. M., & Steinmetz, Z. (2020). Sample Preparation Techniques for the Analysis of Microplastics in Soil—A Review. *Sustainability, 12*(21). doi:10.3390/su12219074

UNEP. (2016). *Microplastics: Trouble in the Food Chain.* Available from https://books.google.si/books?id=WFvjDwAAQBAJ&pg=PA32&dq=Microplastics:+Trouble+in+the+Food+Chain&hl=en&sa=X&ved=2ahUKEwjaoo2D59_zAhX1hv0HHeOUDc4Q6AF6BAgGEAI#v=onepage&q=Microplastics%3A%20Trouble%20in%20the%20Food%20Chain&f=false (Accessed 10. October 2021).

Voukkali, I., & Zorpas, A. A. (2014). Disinfection methods and by-products formation. *Desalination and Water Treatment, 56*(5), 1150-1161. doi:10.1080/19443994.2014.941010

Vriend, P., Hidayat, H., van Leeuwen, J., Cordova, M. R., Purba, N. P., Löhr, A. J., . . . van Emmerik, T. (2021). Plastic Pollution Research in Indonesia: State of Science and Future Research Directions to Reduce Impacts. *Frontiers in Environmental Science, 9.* doi:10.3389/fenvs.2021.692907

Wang, W., Chen, Z., Zhou, Y., Yan, P., Shen, J., Wang, S., . . . Tong, Y. (2021). Catalytic ozonation with silicate-based microfiltration membrane for the removal of iopamidol in aqueous solution. *Separation and Purification Technology, 257.* doi:10.1016/j.seppur.2020.117873

Wolff, S., Kerpen, J., Prediger, J., Barkmann, L., & Muller, L. (2019). Determination of the microplastics emission in the effluent of a municipal waste water treatment plant using Raman microspectroscopy. *Water Res X, 2,* 100014. doi:10.1016/j.wroa.2018.100014

Zioui, D., Tigrine, T., Aburideh , H., Hout, S., Abbas, M., & Merzouk, N. K. (2015). *Membrane Technology for Water Treatment Applications*, Istanbul.

Zirehpour, A., & Rahimpour, A. (2016). Membranes for Wastewater Treatment. In *Nanostructured Polymer Membranes* (pp. 159-207).

Zsirai, T., Al-Jaml, A. K., Qiblawey, H., Al-Marri, M., Ahmed, A., Bach, S., . . . Judd, S. (2016). Ceramic membrane filtration of produced water: Impact of membrane module. *Separation and Purification Technology, 165*, 214-221. doi:10.1016/j.seppur.2016.04.001

Index

M

Membrane filtration · 10, 14, 60

Membrane fouling · 25

Microfiltration · 16, 19, 28, 30, 98, 100

Microplastics · 10, 59, 69, 98, 99, 100, 101, 102

O

ozonation system · 10, 60, 101

R

reverse osmosis · 15, 23, 25, 28, 62, 66, 101

Reverse osmosis · 16, 23, 28, 30

S

SiC membrane · 10, 30, 32, 34, 37, 38, 39, 62, 73, 93

SiC membrane filtration · 10, 30, 62, 93

Sodium hypochlorite · 46

Surface filtration · 11

T

total coliform bacteria · 91, 93

Total nitrogen removal · 83

Total P removal · 86

TSS removal · 79

U

ultrafiltration · 15, 19, 25, 28, 99

Z